INSIDE A HIGH COUNCIL

by

John Larsson

Salvation Books
The Salvation Army International Headquarters
London, United Kingdom

ISBN 978-0-85412-884-6
Ebook ISBN 978-0-85412-885-3

Cover design by Berni Georges.

Project editors: Lieut-Colonel Laurie Robertson,
Majors Sandra Welch and Trevor Howes,
and Paul Mortlock.

SALVATION BOOKS

Published by Salvation Books
The Salvation Army International Headquarters
101 Queen Victoria Street, London EC4V 4EH, United Kingdom

Printed and bound in the UK by Page Bros Ltd, Norwich NR6 6SA

Contents

Preface

THE convening from time to time of a High Council to elect a new General is now part of the Salvationist calendar. In this book I invite readers to step inside a typical modern-day High Council in session to observe what happens. My role will be that of a tour guide, explaining and giving the background to the various facets of the meeting.

My preparation for the role of tour guide has been long and varied. Of the 18 High Councils held to date I have been a member of four – those of 1993, 1994, 1999 and 2002.

I was Chief of the Staff in 2002 and therefore responsible for convening and organising the Council held that year. I was a candidate both in 1999 and 2002 when I was elected General, and have therefore twice personally experienced the process through which candidates pass.

As a member of the 1995 Commission on the High Council, whose remit was to review the criteria for membership of the Council and to consider all aspects of High Council procedure, my assigned task was to look at the way a High Council functions and suggest ways by which the process might be improved.

As General I executed a Deed of Variation in 2005, amending certain provisions in Schedule 4 of the Salvation Army Act 1980 which governs the function of the High Council.

There is furthermore a long family connection with the Council. My paternal grandfather, Commissioner Karl Larsson OF, was a member of the first High Council in 1929, was President of the 1934 High Council, and attended the High Council held in 1939. My maternal grandfather, Commissioner Alfred Benwell, attended the High Councils of 1934 and 1939. My father, Commissioner Sture Larsson, was a member of the High Councils held in 1963 and 1969.

The role and function of the High Council make a fascinating historical study and my original intention was to cover the subject in one volume. However, soon after beginning my research it became clear that the constitutional crisis that triggered the calling of the 1929 High Council needed a book of its own. That volume was published in 2009 under the title *1929 – A crisis that shaped The Salvation Army's future*. The present book completes the project.

John Larsson
General (Retired)

London, October 2013

Chapter One

Genesis

THE eyes of the Salvation Army world are on the closed door of the council chamber where the High Council is meeting. Literally so, for in this 21st century thousands of Salvationists are able to watch the scene live on the Internet.

The High Council, gathered to elect the next General of The Salvation Army, has been in session for many days. Balloting began some hours ago. Word has now been passed out from the meeting room that a new General has been elected. From the northernmost parts of Alaska to the southernmost tip of New Zealand, from the coastal plains of India to the highlands of Kenya, Salvationists wait expectantly. They know the identities of the candidates who have stood for election – but which of them will be the General?

'One certainty,' wrote General Frederick Coutts about High Councils, 'is that there is no certainty.'[1] Of guesswork there has been plenty, but until the door opens no one can be sure.

As the cameras zoom in on the door, it remains stubbornly closed. But not for long. When all is ready the door opens – and the identity of the next General is soon revealed to the waiting world. The joy and warmth with which the new international leader has been greeted within the council chamber is instantly echoed by Salvationists everywhere. When the President prays and asks the Lord to bless the newly elected General, an 'amen' resounds from the far reaches of the globe.

Appointed or elected Generals?

The scene is unique in the Salvation Army world, for, being an army,

The Salvation Army is not given to elections. Officers are *appointed* to their tasks, not *elected* to them. The chain of command is clear and officers receive their appointments from those above them in that chain. The one exception is the General, for no one ranks higher than him or her. The General is therefore the only officer in The Salvation Army who holds his or her appointment through election.

This was not how William Booth envisaged it when he transformed The Christian Mission into The Salvation Army. His plan was that the appointment system would include the General, with each new General being appointed by one standing higher in the chain of command, namely the previous General. This process was set out in the Foundation Deed of 1878. The General-in-office was to place the name of his or her chosen successor in a 'sealed envelope'. This envelope would be opened upon the promotion to Glory of the General, at which point the identity of the new General would be revealed.

The 1878 constitution actually outlined two process options for the selecting of the next General. The incumbent General could either name a successor in the 'sealed envelope' or could leave instructions in the envelope 'as to the means which are to be taken for the appointment of a successor'. While the 'means' in the second option were not defined, it was assumed that the Founder was leaving the elective possibility open, for in the previous constitution – that of 1875 – all future General Superintendents of The Christian Mission (with the exception of William Booth's immediate successor) were to be elected by the Annual Conference of the Mission.

However, in the early days of the Army the focus was entirely on the first option of appointed Generals, with most officers and soldiers not even knowing that an alternative existed. *Orders and Regulations for Field Officers* published in 1886 stated categorically that 'the General must and will appoint his successor', and that was taken as the final word on the matter.

This plan worked only once. When William Booth died in 1912, the 'sealed envelope' that he had handed to the Army's legal adviser for safekeeping 22 years previously was opened in the presence of the Chief of the Staff and a group of commissioners. It was no surprise to anyone to learn that the person William Booth had appointed to succeed him was his eldest son Bramwell Booth, the Chief of the Staff, and he there and then became the second General of The Salvation Army.

Pressure for reform

The concept of a leader of a movement like The Salvation Army having the right to appoint his successor was unusual. In fact, the former British Prime Minister William Gladstone had commented to William Booth in 1896 that not even the Pope could do that. The system began to be questioned in the 1920s and a number of Army leaders pressed for the 1878 constitution to be amended so that future Generals would be elected rather than being appointed.

General Bramwell Booth resisted this pressure for reform. He knew how much thought his father had given to the matter of the succession and felt that the Founder had been divinely inspired in establishing the system whereby Generals would appoint their successors. He also feared that electing the General might have a disruptive effect on the Army. An elective system, he wrote to his sister Commander Evangeline Booth in November 1927, 'would entail delay and uncertainty, and an appreciable if not serious break and stoppage in the control and administration of the Work, and possibly engender personal seekings and rivalries which might break up the unity and spoil the teamwork of the higher command, and even spread downwards, weakening the whole organisation'. He continued:

> Nothing in the whole range of Salvation Army life and growth appeared more important to the Founder than providing – as far as human foresight and wisdom could provide – for the appointment of future Leaders who should be free from the danger of having to rely upon favour, either national or international, in order to obtain or retain their positions. It would be idle to say he did not realise that certain risks

> must attach to any method of appointment, but after long consideration ... he concluded that the method of appointment on which he decided in 1878 ... was, on the whole, the safest and best.[2]

Commander Evangeline Booth, however, spoke for many when in her reply of 9 February 1928 she warned of the dangers inherent in a system whereby the decision was made by one person. 'A group of electors,' she wrote, 'would be far less exposed to the temptation of personal seeking or personal favouritism that is positively inherent in the present system.'[3]

The pressure for future Generals to be elected intensified during 1927 and 1928. But General Bramwell Booth remained firm in his view. He did not consider that he had the power to change the constitution of 1878 – nor did he wish to. He felt that the constitution with its principle of appointed Generals was a sacred trust that had been committed to him by his father, and that it was his duty to preserve it unchanged.

The constitutional crisis

But the pressure for reform did not abate and towards the end of 1928 it burst into a major constitutional crisis, the full story of which I have told in my book *1929 – A crisis that shaped The Salvation Army's future*.[4]

This constitutional upheaval resulted in the summoning for the first time of a High Council of The Salvation Army – a body which most Salvationists at that time had never before heard of. The genesis of the High Council is to be found in the Supplementary Deed of Constitution which William Booth executed in 1904 to remedy some of the deficiencies of the original 1878 constitution.

Among these deficiencies was the fact that the 1878 constitution did not provide a way of removing from office a General who for any reason had become unfit to hold that appointment. 'What if the General were to become a heretic?' Mr Gladstone had asked William Booth. By the 1904 Supplementary Deed the commissioners of The Salvation Army were empowered to remove a General from office for physical, mental or moral unfitness. If the circumstances were clear-cut they did not even have to meet for that purpose. A 'write-in' by the requisite number of commissioners, as specified in the deed, was sufficient.

In cases where the alleged unfitness of the General was not clear-cut or self-evident, the supplementary constitution of 1904 provided for a High Council of senior leaders to be summoned to investigate the matter. Their task would be to adjudicate whether the General was fit or unfit to hold office. If the High Council judged the General to be 'unfit for office' and removed him therefrom, the General's appointment of his successor by means of the 'sealed envelope' became invalid. In such a case the envelope was to be destroyed unopened, with the High Council then having the further duty of electing the next General.

The constitutional provision for a High Council in the 1904 Supplementary Deed was made for the express purpose of dealing with emergency situations that might arise. The High Council was there, as William Booth had said, for the 'possible contingency' of removing a General from office 'who, for some calamitous reasons, had been proved incapable for, or unworthy of, his position'.[5] While the Founder created the provision for a High Council as a necessary constitutional safeguard, we can be sure he hoped the provision would never have to be used and that the High Council would never have to meet.

However, in 1929 the High Council *was* summoned to adjudicate on General Bramwell Booth's fitness for office. A factor in this development was his physical condition. He had not been able to function as General for nine months following a health breakdown. The key factor, however, was the desire for constitutional reform – Generals to be elected and not hold office for life – and the two factors were linked.

If Bramwell Booth were to die, the 'sealed envelope' would be activated and his appointee would automatically and instantly become the next General. This might delay constitutional reform for a generation. But were the High Council to be summoned before he died, the 'sealed envelope' would be deactivated. The trigger for suspending the envelope would be the *summoning* of the High Council, not its convening.

Therefore, when late on a November evening in 1928 it seemed that Bramwell Booth was near the point of death, seven commissioners – the necessary number according to the 1904 Supplementary Deed – hastened the next morning to requisition that the High Council be summoned. The summons went out that same day – 14 November 1928 – and that deactivated the 'sealed envelope'. However, Bramwell Booth survived the night – and well beyond.

The High Council composed of senior leaders met on 8 January 1929. The deliberations of the Council were painful. General Bramwell Booth was held in high regard and no one wanted him to be hurt. He lay ill in his home in Southwold, Suffolk and the High Council sent a delegation to plead with him to enter into retirement, retaining all the honours of his office. But though aged 72 Bramwell Booth was not prepared to do this. After long discussions and a number of adjournments covering a total period of 37 days, the High Council, with great reluctance and sorrow, felt it had no alternative but to adjudicate Bramwell Booth unfit to continue to be General on the grounds of ill health, and voted to remove him from office. The High Council then elected Commissioner Edward Higgins, the Chief of the Staff, to be the next General.

Constitutional reform

The meeting of the 1929 High Council did not change the constitutional situation – at its conclusion the 1878 constitution with its 1904 supplement remained in force. However, the winds in favour of constitutional reform were by now blowing at gale force. Early in 1930 General Edward Higgins therefore appointed an Advisory Commission on Constitutional Reform under the chairmanship of Commissioner David Lamb, one of the Army's elder statesmen, and in November of that year called the first ever

Commissioners Conference to consider the recommendations made by the commission.

The key issue before the Commissioners Conference was whether future Generals would be appointed or elected.

The Advisory Commission on Constitutional Reform recommended that Generals should be elected, not appointed, and this was endorsed by the Commissioners Conference. Even those commissioners who felt strongly that the 1878 constitution should not be changed agreed with the principle of election, recognising that the second 'sealed envelope' option in that constitution already implicitly allowed for the possibility of elected Generals.

The principle of elected Generals is now so well established that it is almost surprising to recall that not all Salvationists at the time agreed with the Commissioners Conference on this point. There was a body of opinion that felt any moving away from the principle of appointed Generals would be a retrograde step. Major Wilfred Kitching – then a young divisional commander but later to be elected General himself – was a forceful spokesman for this view. In 1931, when the United Kingdom Parliament was considering the reform measures proposed in the Salvation Army Act of that year, Major Kitching addressed the Select Committee on Private Bills in the House of Lords. He said:

> The principle of election in the main has never been accepted by The Salvation Army save in certain emergencies as outlined in the [1904] Deed Poll. If you strike a blow at this part of the [1878] Trust you open all other appointments and positions to similar procedure sooner or later. Local officers and soldiers do not dispute the appointment of their corps officer because he is appointed by another. Field officers do not dispute the appointment of their divisional commanders because they are appointed by another. Divisional commanders do not dispute the appointment of their territorial commander because he is appointed by another. Is it not feasible to ask that commissioners shall not dispute the appointment of a future General because he has been appointed by another – in this case the 'other' being the General?

> We have for years made our boast that in many things William Booth was divinely inspired in decisions that he made. Cannot it be accepted that his hand was guided and his mind inspired when he sought to save the Army from a matter that might become abused? Let the decision of William Booth in this matter remain as a trust that is sacred.[6]

Despite such representations the principle of elected Generals prevailed – with the position of General becoming (and remaining) the one and only exception to the principle of appointment within the Army.

A new role for the High Council

Having established the principle that Generals were to be elected, the next question that faced the Commissioners Conference of 1930 was: Who will do the electing?

It was commonly assumed that the electoral body that would be charged with electing a General would be the commissioners of The Salvation Army, not the High Council. This had often been mentioned as the most likely possibility during the constitutional crisis. The commissioners form a clearly identifiable group of the Army's most senior leaders and promotion to the rank of commissioner would then automatically confer the privilege of being a member of the electoral body.

In this scenario the sole function of the High Council would be to deal with any emergencies that might arise – as was the original intention of the Founder. The High Council would be summoned only if there was need to adjudicate on the General's fitness for office, and would elect the next General only if it adjudicated the current General unfit to remain in office.

But after protracted discussion the Commissioners Conference decided not to create a new and separate electoral body to elect the General. Instead, the task would be given to the electoral college already provided for in the constitution, namely the High Council.

Had the decision gone the other way, with a separate electoral body being created, the High Council would have become an historical footnote – an emergency mechanism that was used in 1929, but never since and hopefully never again.

The decision to make the High Council the electoral body charged with electing future Generals did not remove its dual function. To this day, the High Council retains the twin constitutional functions of not only electing the next General, but also of adjudicating, should need arise, on the General's fitness for office.

The principle of Generals being elected, and elected by the High Council, became an integral part of the Army's constitution through the Salvation Army Act 1931, which revoked the relevant paragraphs of the 1878 constitution and enshrined the elective principle in law.

The early fears about introducing the elective principle dissipated with each succeeding High Council. As General Frederick Coutts summed it up in the official history of The Salvation Army:

> There were those who genuinely feared that 'the introduction of the principle of election as a permanent means of appointing future Generals must bring a decay of a General's independence of action, unhealthy rivalry and intrigue, and the eventual disruption of the Army as an international body'. But time has proved these fears unfounded. The international unity and solidarity of the Army is now as strong, if not stronger, than ever. Wisdom was justified of her children.[7]

This book

Since 1929, a further 17 High Councils have been held to date, all of them for the sole purpose of electing the next General. In the pages of this book we will be stepping inside a typical contemporary electoral High Council in order to discover how such a Council works. We will also be charting the developments that have taken place over the years, and will record something of the human drama that is an inseparable part of every meeting of the High Council.

We began by describing the end of the process – the culminating moment when at the end of a High Council the doors of the council chamber are opened and the identity of the next General is revealed to the world. But to observe and get the feel of all that happens when a modern-day High Council gathers in its traditional setting to elect a General we need to enter the door right at the beginning of that process – so, welcome to Sunbury Court!

Chapter Two

Members

THE flags are flying at Sunbury Court as the members of the High Council begin to arrive. They come from the four corners of the earth, the majority of them arriving at the conveniently situated Heathrow airport. They greet each other warmly, and there is a buzz of animated conversation punctuated by bursts of laughter as refreshments are served. At the time of our visit to the High Council the General in office is a married man, and he and his wife – the World President of Women's Ministries – are there to welcome the members.

The settling-in process is quickly accomplished. In the past some members have stayed in a hotel two miles further down the road in the village of Sunbury-on-Thames. But with new residential accommodation built at Sunbury Court – accommodation that will also house the International College for Officers – all members will in future reside at Sunbury Court. The sessions of the High Council will be held in the octagonal conference building constructed in 1999 for use by the Council. All High Councils have been held at Sunbury Court except for those of 1934 and 1939 which were held at the Clapton Centre, and that of 2013 which was held at the Renaissance Hotel near Heathrow because Sunbury Court was being refurbished at that time. As members arrive they check the seating arrangements in the conference room, which are in order of seniority.[1]

Many members have met before at international conferences and at zonal and other more localised leaders' conferences, which are now programmed regularly. In addition, by virtue of being members of the High Council they are all members of the General's Consultative Council, an advisory body to the General that meets under his or her chairmanship three times a year, and have therefore had opportunities to interact with each other in this capacity. These meetings, also held at Sunbury Court, are attended by all commissioners serving at International Headquarters together with representative members from overseas, who come on a rota basis. However, all members take part in every meeting of the General's Consultative Council, even if they are not physically present, as they receive the agenda and minutes electronically and can make submissions.

Pre-High Council conference

The first few days at Sunbury Court will consist of a pre-High Council conference – a plenary meeting of the General's Consultative Council – before the High Council itself is constituted.

Pre-High Council conferences have been part of the pattern from the earliest days. The dynamics of such conferences are unusual in that the General will be leaving office within a few weeks – thus making it inappropriate for important decisions about the future to be taken – and the next General, though as yet unidentified, is on past precedent almost certainly seated somewhere in the conference room. However, such conferences enable retiring Generals to render account of their stewardship and allow key issues facing the Army to be aired. The conferences also enable members to get to know each other at a deeper level. Even at this early stage there will be members who are thought to be potential candidates for the generalship, and though nothing is said openly, any interventions by them in the discussions are especially noted by the other members.

At the first electoral High Council, held in 1934, the conference took place *after* the High Council had concluded, creating the even more unusual situation of both a General and a General-elect being present. The dynamics must have been even more difficult. All eyes would have been on General-elect Evangeline Booth – who would not have had time to master the details of the matters being discussed – rather than on General Edward Higgins who would shortly be retiring. It is therefore no surprise that this pattern was not repeated.

A sign of the greater internationalism of The Salvation Army these days is that not all members of the High Council are fluent in English. The pre-High Council conference gives them opportunity to become acquainted with the provisions made for translation. Members have individual microphones on their desks and everything that is spoken in the council chamber is simultaneously translated into the required languages by the panel of translators located outside the room. The members needing translation hear their language through earphones. When such members wish to contribute to the discussion they simply speak into their desk microphone in their own language and the English translation comes over the loudspeakers in the conference room.

When the pre-High Council conference concludes, the General and his wife leave Sunbury Court. They will meet with the members again when the General leads the public welcome meeting to the High Council, but apart from that have no part to play in the deliberations of the Council until they return to welcome the new General. The joyful public welcome to the High Council is celebrated in a capacious London venue and is one of the high points on the Salvation Army calendar. As the Salvationists present study the photos of the members in the printed programme and look at them seated on the platform, they would be less than human if they did not wonder who the next General might be!

Opening of the High Council

On the morning that the actual High Council opens, it is the Chief of the Staff, as the convenor of the Council in accordance with the Salvation Army Act 1980, who is in charge. The Chief of the Staff leads a time of worship and prayer that from the very opening moment focuses the Council on the spiritual nature of the task for which it has been summoned. Fervent prayers that

God will direct and guide the Council in all of its deliberations are offered by members.

At the conclusion of the time of prayer, the Chief of the Staff draws the attention of the Council to a Memorandum by the Chief of the Staff, *Opening Procedures of a High Council*, and asks the Council to adopt this by a show of hands.

The Chief of the Staff then asks the High Council formally to approve non-member officers who will be present during the deliberations of the Council – usually the recorder, assistant recorder (who in recent High Councils has also been the High Council communications officer), translators, sound system operator, and the legal adviser to the High Council who is on call and attends when needed. The communications officer is responsible for preparing the news releases from the High Council and for responding to messages received by the Council.

The roll is then called, and members respond with 'present' as their names are called. When it is confirmed that all officers eligible for membership of the High Council have been duly summoned, and that only those summoned are in attendance as members of the Council, the person appointed to be the legal adviser to the High Council declares that the High Council 'has been lawfully convened according to the requirements of the Salvation Army Act 1980 as amended by the Deeds of Variation of 1995, 2005 and 2010'.

Membership criteria

A High Council is made up of those officers who, on the 'qualifying date', meet the criteria for membership. The qualifying date normally falls exactly four months to the day before the General is due to retire. All who meet the criteria on that date are summoned to the High Council – even if they are due to retire from active service the very next day. The High Council is usually called to meet about seven weeks after the qualifying date, thus allowing a similar interval after it has concluded its deliberations before the new General enters office.

In a nutshell, the historical criteria for membership of the High

Council have been 'all commissioners and all territorial commanders'. With some minor variations these criteria have remained remarkably consistent throughout the years, the biggest change not coming until February 2010. The membership of the High Council was originally established by the 1904 Supplementary Deed, but changes were introduced in 1930, 1995 and 2010. In this chapter we will look at each stage in turn.

1904 – The original membership criteria

In the 1904 Supplementary Deed the membership of the Council was defined as:

- The Chief of the Staff
- The Secretary for Foreign Affairs
- All the commissioners of the Army not being commissioners on the retired list
- All the officers holding territorial commands in the Army in any part of the world, whatever their rank in the Army.

The Chief of the Staff had separate mention not only because of the status of this position but because in 1904 the Chief of the Staff was not a commissioner. He was plain 'Mr Bramwell'. But this separate mention of the Chief of the Staff has been retained in all subsequent revisions of the membership. Why the Secretary for Foreign Affairs – who at the time was Commissioner T. Henry Howard – merited separate mention is not clear. It was presumably to accentuate the high status of the office – but the office was discontinued some years later and was replaced by one or more International Secretaries.

The 1904 Deed furthermore decreed with respect to the attendance of commissioners and territorial commanders, that when 'two persons being husband and wife, and holding commissions in respect of the same country or district, are entitled to be members of the High Council, they shall only have one vote, which shall be given by the husband as he may think fit if he alone is present or both are present, and shall be given by the wife as she may think fit only if she alone is present'.

However, from this beginning through all the subsequent changes to the membership criteria, it has always been understood that members do not 'represent' the territories to which they are currently appointed, but are members because they are senior leaders.

1930 – Membership criteria changed in the light of the '1929' experience

In 1929 when the first High Council was called, the distinction between 'territories' and the smaller 'commands' was not as clear as it is today. William Booth had decreed in the 1904 Deed that all officers holding 'territorial commands...whatever their rank' should be summoned, and officers in charge of what today would be termed 'commands' were therefore also called. As a result the membership of the 1929 High Council was very diverse and, with seven lieut-colonels and three brigadiers present, ranged from the very senior to the comparatively junior. Considering that the High Council had been called to sit in judgement on the General, this broad range of membership was felt at the time (and subsequently) not to be appropriate.

When the Commissioners Conference met in 1930 one of the pressing agenda items was therefore to restrict the membership of the High Council so that, should a similar situation arise again, the General would be judged only by his or her peers. The Advisory Commission on Constitutional Reform proposed that membership of the High Council should be limited to full commissioners only – excluding even lieut-commissioners. However, the Commissioners Conference felt this to be too extreme, and in the 1930 Deed of Variation (which varied the 1904 Supplementary Deed on this point) the following membership criteria were established:

- The Chief of the Staff
- All the commissioners [including lieut-commissioners]

- All the officers who during the whole of the two years prior to the qualifying date shall have held the rank of full colonel, and shall at the qualifying date be holding territorial commands in any part of the world.

The requirement that territorial commanders who were not commissioners should be full colonels and should have held that rank for two years achieved the intended aim of limiting the High Council to the Army's most senior officers.

When in the early stages of the 1930 Commissioners Conference the option of having a separate electoral body was being discussed, the possibility of extending the electoral body to include 'national and other representatives' was considered. There was even a suggestion that 'this body might be comprised of officers who themselves would be ineligible for election to the position of General'.[2] But once the generic decision was taken that the High Council would have the dual function of potentially adjudicating on the General's fitness for office as well as electing the next General, the emphasis of necessity was on the seniority of its members.

A membership challenge

An unanticipated challenge regarding membership occurred in the run-up to the 1974 High Council. With the unique organisational structure then operative in Great Britain, whereby the heads of the different branches of work reported direct to the General, the Governor of the Men's Social Services, together with the Secretary for Trade at Salvationist Publishing and Supplies, Limited, and the Principal of the International Training College had always been members of previous High Councils. Their attendance had not for a second been questioned – for they had always been commissioners and were therefore clearly eligible on that ground. However, as part of the rethinking about administrative structures in Britain, which was to culminate in 1990 with the creation of the United Kingdom Territory, these three positions were already in the 1970s held by officers with the rank of full colonel. The burning question at the time of the 1974 High Council was therefore whether they were 'territorial commanders' and therefore still eligible to attend the High Council.

The colonels in question presented submissions – one even taking independent legal advice – to the effect that they had the status of territorial commanders and should be summoned to the High Council. These branches of service within the UK, they argued, had always been considered to be 'territories'. Their leaders were governed by *Orders and Regulations for Territorial Commanders*, they reported direct to the General, they had the same powers accorded to territorial commanders – such as being able to promote officers – and the administrative structure of their commands were those of a territory, with a chief secretary or general secretary as their second-in-command.

The Army's legal advisers took the line that, despite the similarities, these branches of services were not in fact 'territories'. However, Commissioner Arnold Brown, who was the Chief of the Staff at the time and therefore responsible for summoning the High Council, decided to refer the question to 'learned counsel' – an expert legal adviser – in order to put the matter beyond dispute. He describes in his autobiography *The Gate and The Light*[3] how he arrived at the Inns of Court to hear counsel's opinion in the midst of a strike by electricity workers. The expert legal adviser handed Commissioner Arnold Brown a 10-page submission which the commissioner read in the faint light of a flickering candle. It ended: 'It is my opinion that the officers in question are not qualified to receive summonses for, or to participate in, the meeting of the High Council.' The point had been clearly made: the officers who had held these positions in the past had been members of the High Council not because of the appointments they held, but because they were commissioners. The leaders concerned accepted this legal verdict with good grace.

It was a unique situation unlikely to arise again. However, in the light of this experience, General Erik Wickberg executed a deed poll which legally designated the territories and commands of The Salvation Army. This list has been continually updated since then by the General of the day executing a new deed poll whenever there is a change, however minor, to the name or status of a territory or command. Only the leaders of the territories (not commands) listed in the deed poll qualify for attendance at the High Council.

The Salvation Army Act 1980

No chronological survey of criteria for High Council membership would be complete without mention of the Salvation Army Act of 1980, even though the Act did not change the membership of the Council. This major piece of legislation revoked the Foundation Deed of 1878 and the Supplementary Deed of 1904 together with the 1930 Variation Deed. It also repealed or amended certain provisions of the Salvation Army Acts 1931 to 1968. With respect to the High Council, the Salvation Army Act 1980 started virtually from scratch and it is now the legislative bedrock on which everything to do with the High Council rests. The details are set out in Schedule 4 of the Act. The General, with the agreement of more than two thirds of the commissioners, has the power to amend Schedule 4 without reference to Parliament.

The Salvation Army Act 1980 retained in Schedule 4 the High Council membership criteria decided by the 1930 Commissioners Conference, namely, the Chief of the Staff, all commissioners and all territorial commanders holding the rank of colonel for two or more years.

1995 – Membership criteria adapted to match a new situation

A major change to the composition of the High Council took place in the 1990s – and it happened without the criteria for membership changing! This remarkable and unexpected development deserves closer examination.

Anyone who has studied the photos of High Councils that adorn the walls of Sunbury Court will have noticed the dramatic difference in the pictures from the 1999 Council onwards. The pictures of earlier High Councils are strongly male dominated, with very few women leaders in them, but from the 1999 High Council onwards women members are present in strength.

Throughout its history the Army has been blessed with outstanding women leaders. William Booth is credited with quipping that his best men were women – and it was not without reason. Many of the largest and most demanding territorial commands have been held by women leaders, as has the leadership of the women's social services and later the combined social services in the United Kingdom. The International College for Officers has also had women principals. At International Headquarters women commissioners have served as international secretaries and heads of key departments. Almost without exception, however, these women leaders have been single officers or widows. The only married woman to attend a High Council prior to the change revealed by the 1999 photo was Mrs General Bramwell (Florence) Booth, who in 1929 attended the High Council because she was a commissioner in her own right. These women leaders, however, have always been a small minority as compared with their male counterparts, a fact that the photos of earlier High Councils clearly reveal.

In 1995 a revolution took place. In that year General Paul A. Rader decreed that all married women officers of whatever rank would hold rank in their own right. By that decision all married 'Mrs Commissioners' would henceforth be commissioners in their own right – and therefore became eligible to be members of the High Council. The consequence of that decision for the membership of the High Council became visible to the whole world when the next Council met in 1999. Furthermore, there was no question of just one vote per couple as the 1904 Supplementary Deed had stipulated. Every commissioner present had a vote.

It is one of the ironies of the history of the High Council that the most radical change ever made to the composition of the Council was a by-product of a policy change that related only indirectly to the High Council. Yet that is how significant advances are sometimes made, for there is no doubt that the increased presence of women leaders has been a positive development.

This sea change in the membership of the High Council required no amendment to the membership criteria set out in Schedule 4 of the Salvation Army Act 1980 to make it effective. Yet General Paul A. Rader, with the required concurrence of more than two thirds of the commissioners, nevertheless amended Schedule 4 in 1995 in order to deal with the new and unique situation of the spouse of a married General-in-office – who would of course be a commissioner in her (and potentially 'his') own right. The dilemma was this: should the spouse of the retiring General be a member of the High Council called to elect the General's successor? A reasoned case could be made either way, but the eventual decision by the General was that the spouse should not be a member.

With Schedule 4 needing to be amended in this way in 1995, it was also decided to take the opportunity to remove the restriction that a territorial commander must be a full colonel and have held that rank for two years. It was felt that this restriction had outlived its usefulness as it was now the practice for territorial commanders to hold that rank. There was also an additional factor. The 'two years as colonel' requirement had, over the years, kept a number of quite senior territorial commanders from attending the High Council, with some of them falling short of the requirement by narrow margins. This was a disappointment not only to the leaders concerned but to the Salvationists of the territories affected. Already in 1934, Colonel Charles Mackenzie, an American officer who had been the territorial commander of the Eastern India Territory for six years and who had attended the 1929 High Council as a lieut-colonel, was ineligible to attend the 1934 High Council because he was 12 days short of meeting the two-year requirement.

With these changes, the membership criteria for the High Council set out in Schedule 4, as amended in 1995, became the following:

- The Chief of the Staff

- The commissioners with the exception of the commissioner who is the spouse of the General
- The territorial commanders.

2010 – A significant change to the membership criteria

It is part of life and development that one change often leads to another. The already noted 1995 policy change in the rank system, by which married women commissioners became members of the High Council, brought in its wake a situation that was increasingly felt to be anomalous with respect to the membership of the High Council.

At the High Councils held in 1999, 2002 and 2006, both spouses of married commissioner couples were present – by virtue of each being a commissioner – but married colonel territorial commanders were there on their own – because territories have only one territorial commander. However, with the passage of time, the view gained ground that in the case of married colonel territorial commanders both spouses should also be present.

With the spouses of colonel territorial commanders not being commissioners and not being territorial commanders, the challenge was to define the status of such officers in a way that made them eligible for High Council membership.

General Shaw Clifton resolved the dilemma in a pragmatic way by a Deed of Variation to Schedule 4 of the Salvation Army Act 1980, executed in February 2010. By this Deed of Variation membership of the High Council was widened to include a third category of officers, namely territorial presidents of women's ministries. This change to Schedule 4 was accompanied by a Minute by the Chief of the Staff which decreed that the term president of women's ministries would in future be applied solely to the spouse of a territorial commander. As a result of these linked twin amendments the spouses of colonel territorial commanders are now members of the High Council.

This widening of High Council membership beyond the traditional 'commissioners and territorial commanders' categories is in fact the most significant change to the criteria for membership of the High Council since the 1904 Supplementary Deed which established the High Council. And with this change the 2011 High Council was the first to have more women than men as members.

In consequence of the Variation Deed of February 2010 the criteria for membership of the High Council are now set out as follows in Schedule 4 of the Salvation Army Act 1980:

> 4. Subject to paragraph 4A below, the High Council shall consist of the following persons: -
>
> (a) the Chief of the Staff at [the] qualifying date;
>
> (b) the Commissioners not on the retired list at such date;
>
> (c) those officers who at [the] qualifying date hold the appointment of territorial commander; and
>
> (d) those officers who at [the] qualifying date hold the appointment of territorial president of women's ministries.
>
> 4A. Neither the General nor the spouse of the General shall be a Council Member.[4]

Further membership factors

The significant change of increased female membership which the photos of successive High Councils reveal has been matched by another transformation. This is the increased membership of leaders from the developing parts of the world – something which is also apparent in the photographs. With more than half of the Army's membership now being in Asia and Africa, it is no surprise that of the 117 members of the 2013 High Council, 19 were Asian and 21 were African.

The photos also reveal the numerical growth that successive High Councils have seen, partly in consequence of the Army's international expansion and partly due to the changes discussed in this chapter. From 1934 until 1994 the average size of a High Council was 46 members. In 1999, with the inclusion of all married women commissioners, membership rose to 74, and with the increased use of the rank of commissioner reached 100 in 2006. With the inclusion of territorial presidents of women's ministries the 2011 High Council had 109 members, and that of 2013, 117 members.

Election of the President

Returning to the contemporary High Council we are observing, when the legal adviser to the High Council has declared that the Council has been lawfully convened and that only those who are legally eligible for membership are present, the Chief of the Staff supervises the election of a President.

The procedures for this election are simple and are set out in the memorandum *Opening Procedures of a High Council*. When the President has been elected, the Chief of the Staff invites him or her to the platform and formally hands over the leadership of the Council.[5] With this action the role of the Chief of the Staff is completed, and the Chief joins the other members in the body of the hall, taking a seat near to the platform as the most senior member present.

For the President, however, things are just about to begin.

Chapter Three

Procedures

HERE and now, without pre-warning or time for preparation, stands the President before the members of the High Council – in charge of everything until the Council accomplishes its mission. Presidents to date have been male, so for simplicity the male gender will be used in this book, but there is absolutely no reason why future Presidents should not be drawn from the ranks of women leaders. The applause that greets the President is prolonged, expressing not only congratulations but also sympathy and hope. As the President waits for the applause to die down he prays inwardly for wisdom. He responds briefly and then moves on to the relatively straightforward task of supervising the election of a Vice-President and Chaplain. He knows that more complicated matters await him, but fortunately there will be a break before he has to face those.

The Vice-President assists in the leadership of the Council and handles practical aspects. The Chaplain arranges the worship meetings and times of prayer. Until the High Council of 2002, Chaplains were appointed by the President, but because of the importance of the Chaplain's role in setting the spiritual tone of the Council, since the 2006 High Council it has become an elected office.

When the Vice-President and Chaplain have been elected the Council adjourns. A key purpose of this break is to enable the President to get his bearings. For that reason the memorandum *Opening Procedures of a High Council* recommends that it should be 'for a minimum of two hours, excluding any meal time'.

Presidents are usually elected from the ranks of senior members and have usually (but not always) attended a previous High Council.

They therefore have a fairly good grasp of what is expected from them. They also, like all members, have received the relevant briefing documentation for the High Council some weeks before. Despite that, most newly elected Presidents probably wish at this point that they had read the material with greater attention. However, the Chief of the Staff, the legal adviser to the High Council and senior members who have attended previous Councils are on hand to offer advice as required.

Procedural guidance

The first document the President consults is the already mentioned Schedule 4 of the Salvation Army Act 1980 (as amended in 1995, 2005 and 2010). This Schedule makes up the 'orders and regulations' for High Councils. It not only sets out the membership criteria but also lays down in broad terms the processes which the High Council must follow. The Schedule has legal force and the President must see that everything in it is scrupulously adhered to.

Just as with the membership criteria, the *procedures* governing the High Council in Schedule 4 of the Salvation Army Act 1980 can be amended by the General, without reference to Parliament, through a Deed of Variation. Any such Deed must have the consent in writing of more than two thirds of the commissioners. As already noted, Schedule 4 has in fact already been amended three times – in 1995, 2005 and 2010.

The second document that the President will reach for is the latest edition of the *Orders of Procedure*. This document amplifies and adds to the points made in the legal Schedule but never contravenes them. It consists of around 70 separate 'orders', short clauses that deal with every aspect of the High Council process – from the appointment of officials and the election of tellers and committee members, to the orders that will govern nominations, questions to the candidates, speeches by the candidates and the actual election of the General. The document also includes two appendices of around 20 points in total dealing with the rules of debate and expenses.

In its original form this document dates back to the first electoral High Council held in 1934. Commissioner David Lamb provided the first draft and many of the paragraphs have remained unchanged from that time. However, each High Council since 1934 has reviewed and refined these orders in some way before formally adopting them. It is therefore the *Orders of Procedure* of the immediately previous High Council that the President will have before him.

Freedom

Schedule 4 declares that 'the persons summoned and meeting as the High Council' have the power 'to determine and regulate the procedure of the High Council'. Every High Council is therefore free to decide how it will go about its business, as long as it adheres to everything set out in Schedule 4. Mr William Frost, the Army's legal adviser, advised in 1939 that 'each High Council is absolutely independent of any other and what has been ruled for one is no criterion for the future'.[1] In theory every High Council is therefore free to reinvent the wheel if it wishes. But in practice that would make no sense. And all High Councils have wisely chosen to build on the experience of previous Councils as contained in the most recent edition of the *Orders of Procedure*.

This freedom has both disadvantages and advantages. A disadvantage is that until a High Council actually meets and a President is elected it does not exist. Of necessity the Chief of the Staff, as the convenor of the High Council, must make practical arrangements such as appointing recorders and translators, but with regard to the more intangible aspects of ensuring a smoothly functioning Council, there is no one the General or anyone else can talk to beforehand. This makes difficult the kind of creative in-depth thinking about the way a High Council functions that might be undertaken in advance and at leisure. Once a High Council has convened, the time pressure is too great for it to stand back and take a philosophical overview of how it functions.

1995 Commission on the High Council

However, a rare opportunity to pause and review came in 1995. In that year General Paul A. Rader set up a Commission on the High Council.[2] Its twin task was to review the criteria for membership and 'to consider all aspects of High Council procedures'. The setting up of the Commission was in response to an undertaking all candidates were asked to give at the 1994 High Council. The forming of the Commission coincided with the announcement that in future all married women officers would hold rank in their own right. There were therefore many aspects to be considered. The Commission gave the *Orders of Procedure* the most thorough review this document had had since the inception of High Councils, and made a number of significant recommendations for consideration by the next High Council. The proposals for change made by the Commission will be noted in the course of this book.

The recommendations with respect to membership made by the 1995 Commission on the High Council were implemented, as mentioned, by the General amending Schedule 4 of the Salvation Army Act 1980. But not even the General had the power to implement the amendments to the *Orders of Procedure* that the Commission suggested. Those could be presented only as *proposals* to the next High Council.

The next High Council, held in 1999, the first at which all married women commissioners were present, adopted most of the recommendations made by the 1995 Commission on the High Council and also made a number of other procedural changes. The 1999 High Council therefore stands as a watershed as far as High Council procedures are concerned. The willingness of that Council to make so many changes was no doubt aided by the fact that 61 of its 75 members were at a High Council for the first time.

A recommendation made by the 1995 Commission on the High Council was that the *Orders of Procedure* should include a clause requesting the Chief of the Staff to convene, within six months of the closure of the High Council, a small Review Committee consisting of the President, Vice-President and some representative members, to review what had taken place at the Council and to leave on record recommendations for the next High Council. This proposal was accepted by the 1999 High Council and the clause has remained in all subsequent editions of the *Orders of Procedure*. A Review Committee has therefore met after each High Council since then, each leaving on record its recommendations to the next High Council. The experience thus far is that most, but not necessarily all, of the recommendations made by such review groups have been adopted by the next High Council.

The advantage of the freedom that High Councils have in determining their own procedures is that significant improvements have in fact been made over the years to the life and function of the Council as the various High Councils have reviewed the *Orders of Procedure*. It would be a bold person who declared that no further refinements could ever be made. Another advantage is that where new circumstances have arisen – for example, the fact that the spouse of a married candidate for the generalship is now present at the High Council – there has been no difficulty in changing the procedures to match the new development.

In this connection it is also important to note that should some unforeseen future circumstance make a major modification to procedures desirable, the General is empowered to amend Schedule 4 of the Salvation Army Act 1980 – with the consent in writing of more than two thirds of the commissioners – so that any and every contingency can be met. All such changes made to Schedule 4 would be binding on future High Councils.

Review and adoption of the *Orders of Procedure*

When the High Council assembles again after the break, the President announces the names of any additional officials he has appointed from the Council's membership.

The President then turns to the next item on the agenda: the review and formal adoption of the *Orders of Procedure* that will guide the High Council in its deliberations. Settling the procedures that will govern the work of the Council is the first major challenge that the President and the members of the High Council have to grapple with. All will have read the sound advice with which the memorandum *Opening Procedures of a High Council* ends: 'In order to preserve the spiritual nature of the Council, the adoption of the *Orders of Procedure* should be undertaken as expeditiously as possible.' All without exception will be in complete agreement with that aspiration.

The copy of the *Orders of Procedure* that the President and the members have before them is the most recent edition as adopted by the previous High Council, together with any refinements the Review Committee may since have recommended. This document sums up the accrued wisdom and experience of all the High Councils that have gone before.

Theoretically the President could ask that the document before the Council be read without comment and then propose that the High Council simply adopts the document as its own *Orders of Procedure*. If that proposal were to be agreed by a show of hands the whole subject would be disposed of in a matter of minutes.

But some form of a review of the *Orders of Procedure*, offering opportunity for questions, comments and suggestions for further refinements, has become a traditional part of the programme of a High Council, and has also been seen as an educational process for first-time members. High Councils usually hope to dispose of this preliminary agenda item quickly so that it can move on to its main task of electing the next General. But dealing with this item 'as expeditiously as possible' has sometimes proved a challenge in practice.

General John Gowans observes in his autobiography *There's a Boy Here* that at the High Councils he attended 'sometimes, it seemed to me, the Council began its work in too leisurely a fashion and completed it at a gallop'.[3] He has a point – and the problem is not new. Commissioner Karl Larsson, who was the President of the first electoral High Council in 1934, comments about that Council in his memoirs *Under Orders* that 'the democratic system allows all the freedom to bring to market their thoughts and whims; and that takes time'.[4]

With High Councils these days having more than twice the number of members than earlier ones, contemporary Presidents need more than twice the wisdom and members more than twice the restraint for matters to flow. Fortunately, unlike most other Salvation Army boards and councils, decisions at the High Council are arrived at by majority vote, as indicated by a show of hands. This enables the President to keep things moving. He does not have to seek to achieve a consensus on every point raised – an impossibility with such large numbers involved. When he considers that some issue has been sufficiently aired in the discussion, he sums up the options and calls for a show of hands. That settles the matter one way or the other and enables the President to move on to the next item.

Over the years the style of discussion at the High Council has become more informal but it is still necessary for the *Orders of Procedure* to be formally proposed, seconded and adopted by a show of hands. In earlier High Councils this was done order by order – a lengthy and tedious process. However, with the orders being grouped in sections within the document, they are now usually adopted section by section, or adopted as a whole at the end of the review of the document.

General Albert Orsborn describes in *The House of my Pilgrimage* his experience of such debates at the second electoral High Council, that of 1939: 'Every single order or resolution had to be proposed and seconded. Often there were amending resolutions. All were thoroughly discussed, before being put to the vote. I personally took a few knocks and tumbles in these debates. Never before had I been obliged to submit to the rules of committee and debate. I jumped and bucked like an unbroken horse!

'I had one interesting debate, where I kept all the rules, and managed to get my amendment carried. I was quite pleased about this, because the debate included a difficult theological point, and it was not thought that my group could win it. But we did, against a very weighty line.

'It took more than this experience to learn how to conduct

myself in a High Council. This Salvation Army convocation has already created its own protocol, which has to be learned; and woe be to the newcomer who offends it, or lets his voice be heard too loud or too often!

'Street corner declamation and even platform techniques are out of place here. A man who knows how to keep silence will learn a lot in a short time, and will afterwards be heard with restrained politeness. But let him declaim or, worst of all, attempt to instruct the Council, and that will mean at least one fewer on all secret lists of possible nominees.'[5]

Election of the Questions Committee and the tellers

When the sections of the *Orders of Procedure* that deal with the election of the members of the Questions Committee and the tellers have been adopted, the President arranges for these elections to take place.

The rules governing the election of the seven members of the Questions Committee are designed to ensure that the group is broadly representative of the various parts of the world. The committee has a complex task ahead of it and therefore gets to work as soon as possible in the proceedings of the Council. The role and function of the Questions Committee in the preparation of the questions that will be addressed to candidates will be described more fully in chapter seven of this book.

Once the four tellers are elected they make a declaration before the Council that they will not at any time disclose the exclusive information which they will acquire as tellers.

Discussions about the Army

One of the *Orders of Procedure* that the High Council considers is entitled 'Committee of the Whole'. It had traditionally read as follows:

> That the High Council shall adjourn as often as necessary to become a Committee of the Whole for the purpose of full and open discussion

> of any subject related to the Army and its mission within the context of the election of a General; that such discussion shall not be subject to voting procedures; that the recorders shall list in the minutes only the subjects discussed.

The first electoral High Council in 1934 tiptoed delicately around the matter of whether it was empowered to discuss issues relative to the position of the General and his responsibilities in leading the Army, and did not even address questions to the candidates. However, in preparation for the 1939 High Council, Mr William Frost was asked to state whether it was proper for the High Council to discuss such issues. He gave clear advice in the *Constitutional Notes* he prepared for the occasion:

> If a High Council thinks (as is really self-evident) that all issues[6] bearing in any way whatever upon the new appointment (which obviously carries with it the Army's most vital future welfare) ought to be fully and exhaustively considered before the appointment is made, then the High Council can discuss them without limit or restraint, and there is nothing that can challenge or stop this. Provided what is done has relation to the new General or his appointment, or the Army's interests in connection with such appointment, the High Council is supreme in regulating its own procedure, and thus saying what shall or shall not be discussed and in what manner the discussion shall take place.[7]

In the light of this advice, the 1939 High Council spent a day, following the completion of its review of procedures, discussing the concept of the General being supported by a 'council' – whether as chairman of a small permanent council (as proposed by Commissioner David Lamb) or by some form of advisory council. However, it seems that the time was not ripe for the establishment of any kind of council, yet a seed had been sown.

The same subject returned at the 1946 High Council, at which Commissioner Albert Orsborn proposed that an Advisory Council to the General be established. This had now become such a vital issue that the High Council devoted three days to its consideration. This time the discussion was conclusive, and resulted in the High Council as a body formulating a question addressed to candidates by which they were asked whether they would be prepared to set up such an Advisory Council to the General.

General Albert Orsborn recalls of those discussions at the two High Councils he attended: 'Before the High Council is established as such, any issue, any matter considered to be relevant to the coming election or to the good of the Army, may be submitted for discussion. If the majority do not wish it discussed it goes into the discard. These discussions are not put to the vote, nor are they based on formal resolution. They are introduced by interested parties and if endorsed, are thrashed out in general debate. Upon them much of the later work of the High Council is based.

'Incidentally, a few days of such debate provide a first-class opportunity for members to assess each other's character, personality, ability and religion. It is quite possible that people who were slow starters may gradually reach a pre-eminent position. It is equally possible that the one in a hurry may talk himself in one day, and talk himself out the next!'[8]

The wording of the Committee of the Whole order allows not only for matters related to the General's responsibilities to be debated, but also for 'full and open discussion of *any* subject related to the Army and its mission' – what General Orsborn termed 'to the good of the Army' – however, with the limitation that such subjects must be 'within the context of the election of a General'.

'These discussions are valuable,' writes General Clarence Wiseman in his autobiography *A Burning in my Bones*, 'because they reveal international trends of thought on important issues and disclose regional differences and problems of which the world leaders should take cognizance. Open debate also assists the Council members in the formulation of those pertinent questions which each nominee for the generalship must answer in writing prior to the election.'[9]

Many High Councils have availed themselves of this provision, usually setting time aside following the completion of the review of the *Orders of Procedure* for such discussions. At some High Councils, however, members have felt that the issues of the day were sufficiently aired at the pre-High Council conference and that no further discussion was needed. At other High Councils members may have deemed that the review of the *Orders of Procedure* had taken longer than expected, and that it was time to get down to the business of electing a General. Or perhaps there was even a corporate sense that the time for further talking was over and that God was guiding the group to move to the election of the General.

In a video interview following his election as General at the 2006 High Council, General Shaw Clifton recalls how 'many subjects were put forward' for consideration in the Committee of the Whole 'but hardly any got discussed because suddenly a hush fell upon the assembled host. As the President announced each item, fewer and fewer people wanted to speak until eventually nobody wanted to speak. Even the people who suggested the subjects didn't want to speak to them. It was very clear that God was saying: "Look, I've enjoyed listening to you speak, but would you please do what you have come together to do. Just do it."'[10]

Length of High Councils

From the first electoral High Council to those of today, the question most frequently asked by those outside the Council is: 'Why are they taking so long?' At the first such High Council in 1934 there was a great deal of press interest because of the dramatic events that had taken place five years earlier in 1929. Commissioner Karl Larsson mentions that around 40 journalists gathered at the Clapton Centre each day, every one of them hungry for news. 'The first bulletins were naturally not very informative,' he writes. 'They had expected the result within 24 hours. And when we could not satisfy them they began to invent news. They informed their papers that we were discussing whether women Salvationists could wear silk stockings and other nonsense that we had never given thought to.

We were split, they said. "The High Council's Dilemma" was a frequent headline.'[11]

This chapter has described what it is that engages the High Council's time and energy, but to convey to the public and even to the Salvationist family the reason for what seems so long a delay has not always proved easy. Salvation Army High Councils are in fact longer than modern-day conclaves summoned to elect the next pope!

However, that depends on how one counts.

When a pope dies or resigns from office the cardinals converge on Rome. On arrival they meet daily in a 'committee of the whole' under the presidency of a senior cardinal. They deal with any church business that cannot be postponed, discuss the priorities for the church and prepare for the conclave that will follow. During this time there will be private exchanges of views between cardinals regarding possible candidates.

Unlike a High Council, a conclave is not free to set its own procedures. The procedures are laid down from on high – by the most recent Apostolic Constitution issued by a pope in his capacity as chief legislator of the government of the church. All Apostolic Constitutions build on what has happened over previous centuries, but usually introduce some modification to the membership of the conclave or to its electoral procedures. Pope John Paul II published such an Apostolic Constitution in 1996. In 2007 and again in 2013 Pope Benedict XIV amended this constitution in small but significant ways by means of decrees.

In their daily meetings before the commencement of the conclave, the cardinals study the details of the current constitution as amended, obtain whatever clarifications they need, and then swear their allegiance to it. The purpose of their discussions is not to amend the constitution but to ensure that they understand it.

It is not until the cardinals process into the Sistine Chapel in the Vatican City on the set day, in the full glare of the world's media, that the conclave as such actually begins, and the clock starts to tick. And after an initial service of worship, all that the cardinals will do in the conclave itself is to reflect – and vote. There are no nominations, speeches or questions. Two ballots are held each morning and two each afternoon until someone achieves a two-thirds majority. This usually happens within a few days.[12] The conclave held in March 2013 lasted two days.

If one counts the length of Salvation Army High Councils in these terms, the picture changes dramatically. In 1934, following five working days dealing with preliminaries, the actual election process was quick indeed. On Monday 3 September 1934 the members met at 10am. Following devotions and attention to some business, the process of nomination began. This resulted in five members accepting nomination. After the nominees had been given some time to gather their thoughts they each addressed the High Council. By 5.15pm the election for General began. Five ballots were held in quick succession and by the end of the evening Commander Evangeline Booth achieved the necessary two-thirds majority, was declared the General-elect and was presented to the waiting press. In conclave terms, the High Council had lasted precisely one day!

The 1946 High Council was the longest electoral High Council to date. It lasted 15 days, which included two weekends. During those two weeks the equivalent of nine full working days were devoted to procedures and Committee of the Whole discussions. The actual High Council process of nominations, speeches, questions and election was accomplished in the equivalent of two full days – Tuesday midday to Thursday midday. Twice as long as in 1934, but nevertheless a High Council of only two days.

So duration depends on how one counts.

However, in a system whereby each High Council sets its own rules, the review and adoption of procedures is an unavoidable part of each Council as those matters cannot be dealt with before it actually convenes. Those responsible for keeping the Army world and the media informed will therefore always have the challenge of explaining that, as with so many things 'Army', The Salvation Army's High Council too is unique in the way that it works.

Yet the picture that General John Gowans paints of High Councils beginning at a leisurely walking pace and ending at a gallop stands as a permanent warning signpost to all future High Councils. Measures have been taken in recent years through the *Orders of Procedure* to ensure that what General Orsborn described as 'the High Council as such' – the real High Council – is not rushed. But with each High Council being unique, the pace that it sets for itself will rest with its President and its members.

Any other business?

When the *Orders of Procedure* have been formally adopted, the questionnaires for candidates have been reviewed and approved by the Council, and any Committee of the Whole discussions have been completed, the President signals that the High Council is about to move into its second and climactic phase by asking: 'Is there any other business to be concluded?'

When that question is met with silence, and not until then, the members know that the High Council has reached its main task and that its next step will be to call for nominations for candidates for the office of General of The Salvation Army.

Chapter Four

Nominations

THE moment the President announces that nominations will now be called for, the weight of personal responsibility that begins to rest on each member becomes almost palpable. There is also a sense of relief. The time for theorising about rules is over. But choices have now to be made. The President reminds the members of the relevant clauses in the *Orders of Procedure* and asks the Council to pause for a time of reflection and prayer. A momentous part of the High Council is about to begin.

Two ballot boxes are placed prominently in the council chamber. The President then begins the nomination process by calling on the Chief of the Staff, as the most senior member of the High Council, to collect his or her nomination paper. The Chief of the Staff proceeds to one of the two voting rooms that are part of the conference centre, writes on the nomination paper the name of the person he/she is nominating, folds the paper unsigned and returns to the council chamber to place the paper in one of the ballot boxes. Before the Chief of the Staff has returned, the President has already called the next most senior member, and as other names are called, a flow of members sets in, with the silence only being broken by the President or Vice-President calling the next name. There is no sense of rush whatever. Members of the Council sit quietly in reflection and prayer until the ballots have been cast. The process can take 50 minutes – sometimes even longer.

The President then calls on the four tellers to count the nominations. The tellers take the ballot boxes to one of the voting rooms where they examine their contents.

The only criterion for nomination specified in the Salvation Army Act 1980 is that the person nominated must be an officer of The Salvation Army. However, according to Schedule 4 (as amended in 2005) only those officers who have been nominated by three or more members of the High Council are deemed to have been nominated. It is therefore only these names that are counted as nominees. The tellers list the nominees in alphabetical order together with the number of nominations each has received.

Some of the nomination papers are likely to be blank. The *Orders of Procedure* have made it clear that members are not obliged to make a nomination. The right to nominate for the office of General is a privilege, not an obligation, and members will have been reminded that if they feel uncertain as to whom to nominate it is perfectly in order to place a blank paper in the ballot box.

The confidentiality declaration made by the tellers at the time of their election has special relevance when it comes to the nomination process in that they may already be able to deduce, from the number of nominations that the various nominees have received, who the next General is likely to be.

The tellers return to the council chamber and the chief teller hands the result to the President. The President scrutinises the list and then reads out the list of nominees in alphabetical order – without indicating the number of nominations each has received.

After a moment for reflection the President announces that the High Council will now adjourn so that those who have been nominated can consider whether or not to accept nomination. He announces the time when the Council will meet again to hear the response from the nominees.

The nomination process is a sacred moment in the life of the Council. It is also a dramatic moment. Behind the nomination process lies history and drama and potential for difficulty that does not immediately meet the eye. To that we now turn.

Selection by nomination

The purpose of a nominating system is to produce a panel of

candidates from which the choice of the next General can be made. Once the candidates have been identified the electoral body is then able to consider the qualities of each and to ask them to participate in the selection process by answering a series of questions and by addressing the Council. This scrutinising would not be possible under a system of direct election.

To have a system of nominations, rather than proceeding straight to the election for General on the pattern of a papal conclave, was the first of three key procedural choices that the 1929 High Council made which set the pattern for the future.

The decision to proceed by way of nominations was not dictated by the legal document establishing the High Council. The 1904 Supplementary Deed of Constitution does not mention nominations but simply says that 'a High Council shall immediately ... proceed to the election of the General'. In choosing to include nominations in the process, the members of the 1929 High Council may have been influenced by the revoked 1875 constitution of The Christian Mission in which nominations were required for the election of General Superintendents by Annual Conference.

The system of nomination is now built into the legal framework through the Salvation Army Act 1980, the fourth Schedule of which states that 'any candidate for election must be proposed by another person being a Council Member prior to the first ballot in which he is a candidate'.

Selection by anonymous nomination

The 1929 High Council made a second fundamental procedural choice when it decided that nominations would be anonymous. Unsigned nominations are in fact unusual in an elective process. The more usual practice is that one or more persons are required to openly nominate someone, often being expected to give the reasons why the person they are nominating should be considered for office.

In the revoked 1875 constitution nominations for the office of General Superintendent were open, and had to 'be made in writing, signed by the parties nominating' 10 days before the meeting of the

Annual Conference at which the election would take place. The 1929 High Council decided not to follow this precedent, and the pattern of anonymous nominations has been maintained by all subsequent High Councils. However, it is not a requirement of the Salvation Army Act 1980 which in its statement that a candidate 'must be proposed' by a member of the Council does not specify the method.

The system of anonymous nominations has certain advantages. A key advantage is that it does not promote competitive 'electioneering' – something William Booth had feared an elective system might engender, and which the 1929 High Council wanted to avoid at all costs. Another advantage is that it lessens the danger of factions forming within the Council – with some, as the apostle Paul might have put it, belonging to Apollos and others belonging to Cephas.

Yet a nomination system that is not open also has its disadvantages. One is that members who make a nomination do not know beforehand whether the officer they nominate will accept nomination. If the person they nominate declines nomination they in a sense have been disenfranchised. An exaggerated example may help to illustrate the point, but the point remains valid even in less extreme situations. If at a High Council there is an outstanding potential General – obviously 'the one' – most members might nominate that person. However, should that person decline nomination for, say, some health reason known only to himself or herself, the majority of the High Council will have 'wasted' their nominations.

No one can know whether this disadvantage in a nomination system that is not open has in fact affected the outcome of past High Councils. But the problem is not hypothetical, for in three of the High Councils held to date more nominees have declined than have accepted – in 2002 six declined and only three accepted – and in a further three High Councils as many declined as accepted.

There are no easy solutions to the problem. Potential nominees can hardly let it be known before the nomination stage of the Council that if nominated they will not accept. That would be thought presumptuous. One possibility, however, would be for members to discreetly and privately ask the person or persons (best in plural) whom they are considering as possible nominees whether they would accept nomination *if* – with accent on the 'if' – nominated. Such personal approaches have undoubtedly been made in the past, but are not without their own difficulties. Members may feel reticent about making such enquiries and the potential nominees may not feel that they can give a clear answer until they discover from the number of nominations received the degree of support that they have in the Council.

Another disadvantage with the system of anonymous nominations is that no statement in support of the nomination is made to the Council. Over the course of the 18 High Councils held to date a number of nominations have been made for which the rationale has not been immediately self-evident. Had the one or more members making the nomination had opportunity to give the reasons why they were nominating that particular officer the picture might have been clearer.

A further disadvantage with anonymous nominations has been the possibility of self-nomination. This matter has now been resolved, but the story is of historical interest. Until the 1963 High Council the *Orders of Procedure* were silent on the matter of whether members could nominate themselves. Whether any had done so in previous High Councils we have no way of knowing, but Commissioner Frederick Coutts felt strongly that this possibility should not be allowed. He writes about it in his memoirs: 'In 1963 I had the temerity to move a resolution that "no member of the High Council shall propose himself or herself as nominee for the office of General". I had raised the point tentatively in 1954, but felt myself so inexperienced among my seniors that I withdrew the proposal without pressing it to a vote. This time I determined to stand my ground. The resolution was seconded, given what was officially described as "very full and lengthy discussion" and was narrowly carried.'[1]

'No officer writes out his own marching orders,' explained Frederick Coutts to his readers. 'Nor can I write my own name in the "marching orders" for the office of General. Others may do that; I must not.'[2]

To later generations it is surprising that the possibility for self-nomination ever existed and that the proposal to close that option was only '*narrowly* carried'. It would seem that there was a considerable body of opinion that felt that self-nomination should remain an option. Self-nomination is now a legally closed option in that Schedule 4 of the Salvation Army Act 1980 states that a candidate must be proposed 'by another person'. In a system of unsigned nominations there can of course be no check on whether someone has nominated himself or herself, but it is inconceivable that a member of the High Council would wish his or her candidacy for the office of the General to be based on a breach of trust. But recent changes in the number of votes required to effect a nomination have anyway eliminated for all time the possibility of someone becoming a nominee by self-nomination – as will be explained in the next section.

In summary it can be said that the disadvantages associated with anonymous nominations are real and difficult to resolve. Yet the system is likely to remain in place, for the disadvantages of open nominations are even greater. It would be virtually impossible to have a system of open nominations without the Council becoming politicised and factions forming. This would be the ultimate negative which High Councils have rightly seen that at all costs they must avoid. Perhaps all of this goes to show that no human system is ever perfect and that it is a blessing that so much can be achieved with systems that inevitably are imperfect.

Selection by a single nomination

The third key procedural choice made by the 1929 High Council was that a single nomination, made by one member, was sufficient for the nomination to be effected.

In this the 1929 High Council did not follow the precedent of the 1875 constitution by which candidates for the office of General Superintendent had to be nominated 'by any twelve members of the last preceding [Annual] Conference'. Twelve was a high proportion of a Conference which at the time would have had only around 50 members. The decision of the 1929 High Council that just one nomination would be sufficient must be considered as unusual for a nominating process. Most nominating systems require at least two – a proposer and a seconder – for the nomination to become effective.

That one unsigned nomination was sufficient to effect nomination opened up not only the possibility of self-nomination, as we have seen, but also increased the possibility of inappropriate nominations without ownership being made.

The potential scope for inappropriate nominations was theoretically vast. The 1904 Supplementary Deed of Constitution decreed that 'the person to be elected may be either one of the members of the High Council *or some other person*' (my italics). That last phrase was astonishingly open. If taken literally, every member of the human race – already in 1904 about one and a half billion – was a potential nominee!

It must have been the prophetic streak in William Booth that impelled him to place no restriction whatever on the High Council in the choice of a General. Yet the openness of the phrase was a danger, especially if linked with a system whereby one unsigned nomination could result in anybody in the world becoming a nominee. Considering that any person so nominated, whoever he or she might be, would have to be asked if he or she accepted nomination, and, if the reply was affirmative, would have to be invited to take part in the High Council, the mind boggles at what might have happened.

However, with the membership of the High Council consisting of senior Army leaders, the danger was always more theoretical than real. In fact, with only one exception the High Council has never yet nominated anyone outside of its own membership. The exception occurred in 1954, when General Albert Orsborn, who had indicated that he wished to retire early, found himself nominated at the High Council called to elect his successor. Nonetheless, the wide openness of the phrase 'some other person' remained a troubling factor in the Army's constitution.

In 1980 General Arnold Brown took action on the matter. The Salvation Army Act of that year restricts the pool of potential nominees for the generalship to the Salvation Army officers of the world. No distinction is drawn in the Act between active and retired officers, but as the mandatory retirement age of the General is 68 the presumption is that only active officers will be nominated. That is still a vast pool of some 17,000 officers in active service, which continues to offer the potential for some unexpected nomination that might prove brilliantly insightful or one that might cause unnecessary delay. However, the constituency from which nominees can be drawn is now much more limited than it was before 1980.

In a further development on the matter of single nominations, the Commission on the High Council recommended in 1995 that, as a safeguard, the threshold for a nomination to become effective should be raised from one to two votes.

Additional impetus was given to that recommendation by the quite separate decision at this time that led to married women commissioners becoming eligible for membership of the High Council. The increased membership of the Council potentially increased the number of nominations, and this gave further reason for the threshold to be raised to two. General Paul A. Rader effected this amendment in 1995 by a Deed of Variation to Schedule 4.

At the 1999 High Council – the first at which married women commissioners were present – the question arose as to whether a member could nominate his or her spouse. As Schedule 4 places no bar on this happening, it was ruled that it was in order for spouses to nominate each other. This in turn raised the question of whether even a threshold of two votes for nominations was high enough.

In 2005 I took the initiative as General to have the threshold raised to three by a further amendment to Schedule 4 through a Deed of Variation. At the time there were those who felt that even three was too low and that it should be five. Their case was that if by the nomination stage of a High Council a person does not have the support of at least five out of around 115 members, that person is unlikely to be able to gain the required votes for election as General by simply answering a number of questions and making a speech. The argument is persuasive, but so too is the argument that the lower the threshold the greater the possibility for some inspired, indeed prophetic, nomination to be made. Perhaps the story has not yet reached its end.

Summary

To summarise this chapter, the three key procedural choices about nominations made by the 1929 High Council continue – with slight variation – to determine how a contemporary High Council works today. Candidates have first to be nominated, nominations are anonymous, and the threshold for nomination is low – but has risen from one to three.

The drama of nominations, however, does not lie in the process but in the people involved – those who have to make the nominations, and those who find themselves nominated. These twin aspects will be considered in the next two chapters.

Chapter Five

Nominators

AS the members of the High Council leave the council chamber following the President's announcement of the nominees, they clutch for further reading and reflection the list of names that they have jotted down. The *Orders of Procedure* specifically mandate that there must be a period for 'private prayer and meditation' to allow the nominees to weigh their decision.

The list of nominees can be long. The 1986 High Council - at which General Eva Burrows was elected - still holds the record for the number of nominees. At that Council of 46 members, 13 of them were nominated. The smallest number of nominees - only four - was at the 1977 High Council when General Arnold Brown was elected.

When the members look at the list of names they note whether the name of the person they nominated appears. If the name is not on the list they know that the threshold of three votes was not reached. They also note any unexpected names. It is not unusual for some nominations to be surprising, even baffling. They also look for the surprising omissions. In many High Councils members who would seem to be obvious choices fail to be nominated. Perhaps the individuals concerned are also surprised, maybe even disappointed, but any such reactions remain well hidden. Members also begin to wonder which of the nominees will accept nomination and thus become candidates.

For some members, being cast in the role of a nominator has not been an easy experience.

Identifying potential nominees

At an early High Council I attended a colleague of mine from a distant part of the world asked me an unexpected question. We had been friends for many years, from the time that our Army service first brought us together, and had often shared in deep conversation. 'John,' he said, 'I really don't know who to nominate. Have you any thoughts on the matter?'

The question was delightfully frank and pointed. But I knew that one of the *Orders of Procedure* states that 'there shall be no speeches or conversation at any time by members in advocacy or otherwise of any nominee or candidate'. Even without that clear rule I would have felt it out of place to try to influence my friend towards any particular choice. I therefore took the chance to remind him that he was not obliged to make a nomination – a point which had not yet been made entirely clear at that High Council – and I can still remember the look of relief on his face.

I also knew that once actual candidates had been identified it would be easier for my colleague. It would then be a matter of choosing between Candidates A, B or C, and by then there would be a basis of information about each candidate on which to make a judgement.

The dilemma that my friend faced at the nomination stage is one that many former members of a High Council would recognise. With more than 100 possible nominees within the Council and potentially another 17,000 beyond its borders, how does a member know who best to nominate? General Albert Orsborn referred whimsically to the 'secret lists of possible nominees' that members might carry in their heads or even on paper. However, for some members the problem is that the list is either blank or has a number of names but with no one name standing out above the others.

Heart and head

Singling out the right name will be for members partly a matter of the heart. In seeking to identify the right nominees and then, at a later stage of the Council, the right General, members of a High

Council are engaging in an exercise of spiritual discernment. Together as a group and each individually, the members are asking God for wisdom and guidance in order to discern who should be the next General. For that reason there is great emphasis on corporate and personal prayer throughout the duration of the High Council. This is even more so on any Sunday that occurs during the Council, for business has not usually been transacted on the Lord's Day. And the turning to prayer happens not only at Sunbury Court, for the whole Salvation Army is at prayer, with messages received to that effect being shared with members during the course of the Council.

The intensity of spiritual seeking in the devotional times at a High Council often remains a highlight memory for those who have been members. General Arnold Brown recalls in his autobiography: 'The procedures of the High Council in selecting an international leader for the Army are more a spiritual exercise than the employment of ordinary electoral processes. The incomparable fellowship, heightened by much prayer and reading of the Scriptures, has all the features of a highly devotional spiritual retreat. Imperceptibly, appraisals of possible nominees are shaped and, as voting time draws near, a sense of guidance, flowing from the Holy Spirit's presence, possesses the delegates' minds and hearts.'[1]

However, appraising possible nominees will also be a matter of the head. Members individually or corporately as a Council cannot only spend time in prayer and hope that through the supernatural guidance of the Holy Spirit the identity of the next General will somehow crystallise in their minds. That, it seems, is not how God chooses to work. St Augustine's famous saying that 'without God we cannot, but without us God will not' applies also to the task of a High Council. Those taking part in an exercise of spiritual discernment must apply their minds as well as their hearts to the task before them.

Members of a High Council will therefore be seeking to define in their thinking the kind of qualities they are looking for in a potential General. Vatican watchers have coined a word for those cardinals who are considered to have the makings of a pope. The word is *papabile*. It is an Italian word, but which is now used internationally, meaning 'has pope potential'. Ever since arriving at Sunbury Court, and even long before, the members of the High Council will have been assessing in their minds which Army leaders have the potential to be General. Some members may even have extended their mental search beyond the ranks of the High Council itself.

Mix of factors

There is no such thing as a profile of a potential General. Having the makings of a General depends on a mix of factors that are almost impossible to define. These have to do with qualities of heart, mind and spirit, with giftedness and ability for the task, and with past experience and achievements. One has only to look at the personalities of the 20 Generals the Army has had thus far to see that there are as many differences of qualities as there are similarities. Such differences will be reflected in the pool of potential nominees at a High Council. What one can bring to the task will often be in sharp contrast with what another can bring, and as the High Council cannot meld their best qualities into a single perfect candidate who has everything, it finds itself having to make a choice between people with very different gifts – but who each has the potential to be General.

The choice, furthermore, is often influenced by what the High Council feels is right for that particular point in the Army's development. In the Army's history there appears to have been a distinct pattern of Generals being chosen because it was felt that what they could bring to the office of General was just what was needed for the circumstances of that time.

The classic case was the High Council of 1939. After William Booth, Bramwell Booth, Edward Higgins and Evangeline Booth, who each in his or her way had been a towering figure bestriding the scene, there could not have been a more surprising choice than that of the low-key, almost shy, Commissioner George Carpenter. But the 1939 High Council, hearing in the distance the sounds of preparation for war, felt that no one among them was better qualified to head the Army in what was likely to be a time of outer turbulence than George Carpenter. 'The High Council,' writes Stella Carpenter, his daughter biographer, 'turned towards one, distinguished not for notable ability, nor eloquence, but for godliness, courage and a steady quiet faith in God.'[2] No one has ever doubted that the Council made the right choice.[3]

The age factor

Another factor in considering potential Generals is that of age. To be considered, a nominee must be neither too old nor too young. At the top end of the age range, a General must be able to serve a reasonable length of time before reaching the mandatory retirement age – with what is seen as reasonable being left to the discretion of each High Council. Since the introduction of a set age of retirement for the General in 1932, the retirement age has gone from 73 to 70 and now stands at 68.[4]

The General elected with the longest term prospect before reaching the age of retirement was Commissioner Albert Orsborn. He could have served as General for 10 years and three months, but decided to retire after eight years in office. General Wilfred Kitching is therefore the General elected by a High Council who has served the longest term – nine years and four months. The General elected with the shortest term prospect has thus far been General Clarence Wiseman, who served for three years less two days before reaching the mandatory retirement age.

With regard to the lower end of the age range, a potential nominee who is thought to be too young is less likely to be considered – though on this point further comment is necessary.

Earlier High Councils seemed reluctant to elect younger Generals – probably for the understandable reason that the person they elected might be around for too long. What if the Council had got it wrong? To seek to remedy this problem General Clarence Wiseman, with the concurrence of more than two thirds of the commissioners, introduced in 1975 a set term of five years for Generals – unless the General reached the mandatory retirement age before the end of the term. It was hoped that having a five-year term would encourage High Councils not to overlook potential younger nominees because of their age.

In a complementary development, also with the support of more than two thirds of the commissioners, General Jarl Wahlström in 1986 introduced a system whereby a General's five-year term of office could be extended by one, two, or three years by means of an anonymous postal ballot of those eligible for membership of a High Council. With the development of technology, and given the consent in writing of two thirds of the commissioners, such a ballot could in future be conducted electronically. An extension to a General's term would need the support of more than two thirds of the members of the High Council.

In both of these changes the Army re-adopted features of the revoked 1875 constitution under which General Superintendents were to be elected for a five-year term which could be renewed. General Eva Burrows is the only General thus far whose term of service has been extended through such a ballot. She was 61 when her term of office was extended for a further two years.

By a gradual evolution the Army has arrived at a flexible system which potentially allows for the election of younger Generals. Should another William or Catherine Booth arise in our midst, he or she could be elected General at an early age, could serve for a term of five years, and could then have his/her term extended by postal ballot of the High Council for up to three years. After this maximum interval of eight years the High Council would have to physically meet. It would, however, be constitutionally possible for the outgoing General to be nominated and elected again at that High Council and five years later to have his/her term extended for up to three years by a postal ballot of the High Council. There would be no constitutional bar to this cycle of election and extension being repeated until the General concerned reached the mandatory retirement age.

It is even possible for a General's term to be extended beyond the mandatory retirement age, but the relevant regulation includes the wise proviso that this 'shall not normally' be considered.

All these factors regarding right qualities and age will be in the minds of the members of the High Council as they consider possible nominees for the office of General. However, in the process they will each have come up against the biggest problem of all – namely the lack of knowledge that they have about the possible nominees, not only about the 17,000 out there but about each other as well.

The dilemma of lack of knowledge

When my friend at the High Council was unsure about who to nominate, I fully understood his predicament – and also knew that the root of his dilemma was this lack of knowledge about the potential nominees. I reflected on this when it came time for me to nominate someone at that same High Council, for I had to admit to myself that the nomination I made was as much based on intuition as on knowledge.

The members of the first two High Councils – those of 1929 and 1934 – had no such dilemma. This was a time when the giants who dominated the scene had been around for a long time. To take but one instance, by the time of the 1934 High Council Commander Evangeline Booth had been the USA National Commander for 30 years, and prior to that had been the territorial commander of Canada for eight. Commander Evangeline needed no introduction; her record and achievements spoke for themselves.

However, already by the next High Council in 1939, as General George Carpenter's biographer comments, 'there was no obvious choice in the field'[5] and such was the mutual lack of knowledge about each other that one member had actually to request that they at least be provided with each other's birthdates before it came to nominations.

Since 1939 the turnover of senior leaders has accelerated, and the comparatively short time that leaders these days spend in senior leadership has made it even more difficult for them to get to know each other at depth and for potential nominees to emerge. Nowadays, many do not qualify for High Council membership until their final appointment before retirement.

Resolving the dilemma of lack of knowledge about potential nominees is not easy. Perhaps a fully satisfactory resolution is impossible.

Some doors to fuller knowledge have rightly been closed. As already noted, the early High Councils were right to rule out open nominations. A system whereby nominees had to be openly proposed, and perhaps even seconded, in say 10-minute speeches, would certainly help to diminish the knowledge gap about nominees and would especially provide a way for the merits of little known nominees to be brought to the attention of the Council. However, as mentioned, the danger of the Council breaking into factions would be too great.

The early High Councils were also right to frame the rule that advocacy would not be permitted in the deliberations of the Council. But such a stand carries a price in that members are denied the kind of information about potential nominees that would be available to electors in, say, a political election. Yet the danger of turning the High Council into a worldly competitive contest would be far too great, and it is therefore right that the 'no advocacy' rule has been retained.

The Army's leadership was also right to rule out in the early 1930s another way of resolving the problem of lack of knowledge – namely that the outgoing General should have the right to submit to the High Council 'the names of not more than three officers whom he thinks suitable for consideration'[6], but without the High Council being limited to those names. The suggestion was made by the Advisory Commission on Reform which was grappling with the transition from appointed to elected Generals. The Commission felt that the General was in a position to know potential successors better than anyone else. Was it therefore sensible to exclude the General completely from the new electoral process?

For the High Council to know the mind of the General-in-office would without doubt be a valuable starting point for many members. Yet at the Commissioners Conference in 1930 there was little support for the idea of up to three officers being openly singled out in an otherwise anonymous nomination process. It was also felt that the persons concerned might not appreciate being so closely identified with the outgoing General. The suggestion therefore did not even reach the 1934 High Council.

It was right that the proposal was not pursued, but that does not mean that the General-in-office has no role. On the contrary, his/hers is the vital role of ensuring that there is always in existence a body of experienced leaders with the potential of being the next General. With the pattern of Generals being chosen from within the High Council, it is the General who determines the pool from which the potential nominees will be selected. The General therefore has a crucial role in the election process.

Ways of gaining knowledge

Though some doors to gaining more knowledge have rightly been closed a great deal has, in fact, been done since the 1939 High Council to enable Council members to know each other better.

At all High Councils since then individual photos and a brief biography of every member have been provided. These write-ups are prose versions of the official service record of members, giving key dates, lists of appointments held, details about marriage and family, etc. They are masterpieces of objectivity and include no value judgements whatever – no one's service has been 'outstanding' or even just 'faithful'. The summaries deal only with basic facts.

The possibility of amplifying these résumés into more extensive biographical notes has been considered – and rejected. Not even Solomon in all his wisdom would be able to write such in-depth pieces without a degree of advocacy or counter-advocacy creeping in, even if only subliminally.

Members' knowledge of each other has also been increased in successive High Councils by more extensive use of the Committee of the Whole provision for the discussing of issues. Reflecting the situation as he saw it in 1974, General Clarence Wiseman writes: 'The cut and thrust of unfettered discussion elicits a wealth of information about the councillors themselves that serves to augment available biographical data. This is exceedingly important. In every High Council some officers are present for the first time. Not a few are comparative strangers to one another, never having met in such intimacy before; others are complete strangers, having never met before. To make intelligent choices they must get to know each other before nominations.'[7]

The greatest advance in the closing of the knowledge gap since 1939, however, is the many opportunities that Army leaders today have for meeting together for conferences. As previously noted, international conferences of leaders presided over by the General are now held regularly, as are zonal conferences, also chaired by the General or the Chief of the Staff. More localised conferences in which groups of territorial commanders meet are also frequently held, often annually, and these enable at least some of the members to get to know each other better.

Despite these various provisions for members to meet together, as recently as at the 1999 High Council one commissioner made the point just before the nomination stage that, because he had not been to an international conference of leaders nor a previous High Council, he knew less than a quarter of the members of the Council. He appreciated the opportunity there had been to get to know members up to that point in the proceedings. However, in approaching nomination time he found that he still lacked knowledge of members' passion for mission and zeal for the Kingdom of God. He therefore made a plea that in future High Councils, before the time for nominations was reached, members should have a chance to speak of their work, hopes and fears in a form which would reveal their hearts, and so allow equal emphasis on passion and mission to that placed on procedures.

Since the 1999 High Council the opportunities for members to interact at conferences has increased even further with all members of the High Council being members of the General's Consultative Council. This affords them occasion to meet from time to time and also to be informed about each other's views and opinions by electronic means. Yet the challenge remains. For even periodic encounters in a conference setting do not necessarily reveal the full heart of a person or his or her 'passion for mission or zeal for the Kingdom of God'. There will still be large gaps in knowledge.

Individual responsibility

Reducing the knowledge gap in the approach to a High Council will, to a large extent, depend on individual members proactively seeking to be as well informed as possible about potential nominees. This quest for knowledge is for every member an inescapable duty.

Some weeks before the High Council when the members receive the list of its membership together with the individual photos and mini-'bios', they will prayerfully consider each person in turn. Some members will immediately stand out as possible nominees by virtue of the appointments that they hold. Among these will be the Chief of the Staff, who by virtue of his/her office will be one of the few persons known to all. It is no surprise that the Chief of the Staff has been nominated in 16 of the 18 High Councils held thus far. The previous appointments that each member has served in and the kind of experience and international exposure he or she has gained will be closely scrutinised. Some members will be known from personal contact at conferences and congresses. Some will be known from their writings – or from their postings on the Internet. Others may be almost totally unknown. A provisional mental list of potential nominees often begins to form, but always with the thought that the right name may not yet be on it.

It has not been unusual for members to engage in pre-High Council correspondence or conversations about the kind of General the Army needs for the circumstances of the times. In the lead-up to the 1939 High Council, Commissioner George Carpenter (Territorial Commander, Canada) was in correspondence with a number of leaders. He wrote to one: 'I am anxious that the new

General shall, by simplicity and sacrifice recapture much that has been lost in the years.'[8] To another: 'I know the kind of man I think the Army needs, but where or who that man is, is not clear to me.'[9] To Lieut-Commissioner Albert Orsborn, the young territorial commander for Scotland, who he thought might be the man, he wrote: 'I should want my man of destiny to be a man of passion for Christ – of aggressiveness in action – pronounced in his experience and proclamation of holiness, and fervent in regard to the salvation of old and young. I should want him to be big enough to take and maintain a lonely walk if necessary.'[10]

In such correspondence or conversations – whether before or during the High Council – a clear distinction has sensitively to be drawn between advocacy and a search for light. The High Council is like an appointments board charged with filling the most vital appointment for the Army's future. Its members have a sacred responsibility to gain as much information as they possibly can on which to base their eventual judgement. In more recent times the relevant clause in the *Orders of Procedure* has been reworded to recognise this fact. After stating that 'there shall be no advocacy or otherwise of any nominee or candidate' in speeches and conversations, it adds: 'However, members may in personal conversation discuss the qualities of potential holders of the office.'

But should any member seek to campaign, however subtly, for or against a particular nominee, he or she would soon feel the disapproval of the group. Such an approach would be entirely out of keeping with the spirit of a High Council. Seeking for knowledge, yes. Advocacy, no. Having to maintain the fine and sometimes difficult distinction between the two is an unavoidable part of a system which combines an elective process with a spiritual process. General Frederick Coutts writes about the High Council system:

> Though this procedure is described – for want of a better term – as an election, nothing is less like an election in the ordinary usage of that word ... The atmosphere of the hustings is replaced by a spirit of

> prayer. Without doubt members hold their several views as to who should be elected, but there is no wheeling and dealing. I can testify that my vote has never been solicited, neither have I at any time solicited a vote for myself or anyone else, nor have I ever voted for myself.[11]

In the representative High Council into whose life we have stepped, the nominators, despite the challenge of imperfect knowledge, have nevertheless made their nominations. The process of heart and mind that led them to their choices is now in the past and the result is known.

What are the thoughts and feelings of those who discover that they are now nominees for the office of General of The Salvation Army?

Chapter Six

Nominees

THERE is a distinct air of expectancy as the members of the High Council return to the council chamber following the adjournment granted for the nominees to decide whether or not to accept nomination. The President will shortly ask each of them in turn to respond.

In two previous High Councils not all nominees were present at this point in the life of the Council to give their responses in person. In 1939 the Chief of the Staff, Commissioner John McMillan, and Commissioner Samuel Hurren (Principal of the International Training College) were absent due to illness, yet both were nominated. The President arranged for each to be visited by two members of the Council in order to ascertain their answers and the deputations returned with letters from them in which each declined nomination. Commissioner John McMillan died four weeks later. In 1954, as already mentioned, General Albert Orsborn was nominated at the High Council convened to elect his successor. When informed, he too declined.

If others from outside the High Council should be nominated in the future, the *Orders of Procedure* are clear. The President is to inform them of their nomination, obtain their response, and if affirmative, invite them to make their way to Sunbury Court as quickly as possible in order to take part in the High Council's proceedings.

The length of the adjournment for nominees to decide whether to accept or decline has gradually been extended with successive High Councils. Nominees are faced with a momentous decision.

Acceptance will not only mean that they may have to assume the burdens of the generalship but in many cases will involve them serving for additional years before reaching retirement. Such factors, especially for those who find themselves unexpectedly nominated, raise questions that need careful pondering. A married nominee will want to discuss the issues at depth with his or her spouse.

It is therefore almost surprising to discover how quickly the nominees were required to make up their minds in the early High Councils. For example, the 12 nominees in the 1946 High Council, some of whom would have received their nomination with surprise, were given precisely 20 minutes to decide. Later High Councils recognised the need for the nominees to be granted more time and, with the increased facility for international telephone calls, the *Orders of Procedure* eventually decreed that the adjournment must be long enough for nominees to be able to consult their spouses by telephone.

Contemporary High Councils, at which spouses are present, allow nominees adequate time for reflection and consultation before they have to make their response. 'This period to be not less than four hours, or longer at the discretion of the President,' state the *Orders of Procedure*.

The *Orders of Procedure* also take very seriously the matter of both spouses being in agreement with the decision. The relevant paragraph reads: 'In the case of a married officer accepting nomination to the office of General, the spouse shall be asked to assure that he/she is in accord with the spouse's decision to stand for election.'

Another way in which procedures of High Councils have become kinder to nominees in the sometimes difficult decision they have to take, is that they are now authorised by the *Orders of Procedure* to ask the President privately during the adjournment how many nominations they have received.

This was not so in the early High Councils. At those Councils the tellers handed to the President a list of all the nominees in alphabetical order, but without any indication of how many votes each nominee had received. From 1969 onwards, however, the tellers were instructed by the *Orders of Procedure* to provide an additional list with the names of those who had been nominated by three or fewer (later five or fewer) members, and the President was authorised to disclose privately to any inquiring nominee whether their names were on that additional list.

The reforming 1999 High Council considered that even this provision was insufficient for nominees faced with the decision of whether or not to accept nomination. The Council felt that it was in the interest of both the nominees personally, and the High Council as a whole, for the nominees to know the actual number of nominations they had received. The Council therefore amended the *Orders of Procedure* and the tellers were instructed to include on the alphabetical list of nominees the number of nominations each had received, and authorised the President to make known privately to any nominee who enquired the number of nominations he or she had received. This ruling has been maintained by succeeding High Councils.

The information about the number of nominations received can be an important factor when nominees consider their response. Some nominee might discover that he or she has been nominated by enough members to make eventual election likely, whilst another may discover that nomination is by the barest minimum, making eventual election a more remote possibility. However, it is not mandatory that nominees enquire, and not all nominees avail themselves of this provision, some feeling that the fact that they have been duly nominated by at least three of their colleagues is a sufficient basis on which to accept nomination.

The human drama of saying 'Yes'

A number of Generals have recorded in their memoirs their thoughts and feelings when faced with the decision whether or not to accept nomination. Their personal sharing reveals not only the human drama of the moment but also the many and diverse factors that such a decision may involve.

General Albert Orsborn wrote movingly, with the insight and descriptive power of a poet, about his experience of the 1946 High Council at which he was elected General:

> For myself, I felt the seriousness of the actual nomination as the time approached. I knew it was coming, but from whom I could not say. I thought I was mentally and spiritually conditioned to meet it. Yet, in that solemn and pregnant moment, I trembled ...
>
> Nomination did not solemnise me as much in 1939 as it did in 1946. In the interval I had looked more deeply into its implications. It had come home to me that all my previous appointments had been decided by my leaders. I had not been consulted about them; I had accepted them without question.
>
> But now I was being asked to say 'Yes' or 'No' to a nomination which might lead to the heaviest, most responsible post of all. It made me think. I had always received marching orders, written and signed by my responsible leaders. This had been a strength to me. If elected, who would give me my appointment?
>
> Then I apprehended the inexpressible demand of a worldwide Army for spiritual leadership...I knew that election would mean that the host of God would be looking to me. They would expect me to be always the man with a message. The thought made me tremble. The General is not merely the titular head of an organisation, he inherits a spiritual trust which is not just a repository of ideals but is a tradition of vision, inspiration, holy example and dedication to God.
>
> Another more personal hesitation arose from my disinclination to travel. I had never liked it, preferring home and the quieter ways. I especially disliked flying. I was never any good at heights! The idea of being constantly on the wing, or aboard ship, did not appeal to me. This was, however, counterbalanced and compensated by my passionate love of people. I did not want to see places, but if by travel I could reach our precious Salvationists, and carry the salvation message to countless thousands, I would do it. Perhaps an even deeper change within me, since 1939, because of inexpressible sorrows, [Albert Orsborn had been widowed for a second time] made me reluctant to accept new burdens.

I took these matters, with others, to God in prayer during the interval in Council business. I wanted to say 'No'. Only a conviction that I must accept nomination, carried me forward. In my life I have heard a great deal about people receiving absolute divine guidance and assurance in coming to decisions. I cannot truly say things have gone like that with me. More often than not, it has seemed that God drove me back upon my own knowledge of the facts, and upon my own willingness to take a decision, and step out in faith.

It was so at the High Council. No new or dramatic revelation was vouchsafed to me. As I prayed a settlement and peace came to me. I looked up to God and told him of my complete inability to do anything without him. Then – and only then – I received my text: 'In quietness and confidence shall be your strength'.[1]

General Erik Wickberg recalls in *Inkallad* (*Called Up*) that it was with 'great reservations' that he accepted nomination at the 1969 High Council, which elected him as General. He expands on those reservations when writing about the 'mixed feelings' he experienced following election. 'Now it would be another five years before we could return home to Sweden [he had been the Chief of the Staff for nine years, and prior to that the territorial commander for Germany, and before that the chief secretary for Switzerland]. Many long journeys around the world lay ahead, with heavy meeting programmes. I have said more than once that had I not had the long period as Chief of the Staff I would hardly have felt up to the task.

'The purely administrative side of the generalship I was well acquainted with, but to take on such a responsibility at that age [Erik Wickberg was 65 at the time and the retirement age for Generals was then 70] can undoubtedly appear quite rash. To be sure, both Gretel and I were in good health, and hoped to get through these five years in vigorous physical and spiritual form.'[2]

In *En Vallfartssång* (*A Pilgrim's Song*) General Jarl Wahlström refers to the affirming influence of his wife Maire at key turning points of his life. He highlights her role when writing about his nomination at the 1981 High Council at which he was elected General:

'It had been agreed that every candidate should make contact with his wife to make sure that she too supported the matter. Generalship involves greater obligations and burdens for each of the partners. So I phoned Stockholm [Jarl Wahlström was the Territorial Commander for Sweden at the time] and informed Maire that I had been nominated.

"What do you think? Should I accept nomination?"

Maire thought for a moment and then said:

"You must decide for yourself. But I am not against it."

So once again Maire had said "yes" without really knowing what it would involve.'[3]

In his biography of General Eva Burrows, *General of God's Army*, Colonel Henry Gariepy describes how following nomination at the 1986 High Council, at which she was elected General, 'Eva retired to her room to pray. She monitored her motives. "Do I want to accept this because it would be the crowning pinnacle of my life? Do I want this to show that a woman can do it?" Having crystallised and chastened her own motives, she was led to an awareness that it was right for her to accept nomination.'

'"When I accepted nomination, I did not say to myself, 'That means you're going to be in, you're going to be the General.' No, I think I was very prepared, saying, 'Lord, I am ready to be accepted, but if I am not, it's all right.' I was so happy in Australia [Eva Burrows was Territorial Commander of the Australia Southern Territory at the time] and really enjoying that demanding leadership role. I would have been perfectly happy to go back...So I was at peace whatever the decision."'[4]

At the 1994 High Council the then Commissioner Paul A. Rader, Territorial Commander of the USA Western Territory, found himself being considered a very obvious candidate to be the next General. He had been the one other candidate remaining in the field in the final ballot at the High Council held the previous year. In her biography of Paul A. Rader and Kay F. Rader, *If Two Shall Agree*, Carroll Ferguson Hunt picks up the story, based on her interviews with them, from when the unexpected vacancy in the office of General became known:

> One or two people made the comment, 'Well, you're next.' But neither Rader was looking for promotion. The West was a wonderful place to be, and going through the election process again held no charm whatsoever. Paul turned aside their well-meant comments by saying, 'You're very kind, but that remains to be seen, doesn't it?'
>
> Just days before he left [for the High Council], Kay and Paul spent a day hidden away in a motel room in California, a day of praying, reading, thinking, talking.
>
> 'We were not at all sure if Paul were nominated that we wanted to accept,' Kay says. 'We had settled in to go on with MISSION 2000 there in the West…I perhaps more than Paul considered what it would do to our family.' Kay knew that it would entail a loss of privacy for their children and grandchildren, creating a vulnerability to public scrutiny they did not choose. And for both Kay and Paul, a nomination would require them to face the possibility of a second highly visible and much discussed rejection, a prospect most difficult to contemplate. Paul says his reluctance centred around questions concerning what the Lord wanted.
>
> 'If God didn't want you in 1993, why should he want you in 1994?' he said.
>
> How did they resolve these questions? 'We prayed on our knees all day,' Kay says.
>
> Paul knew that 'it was important we both be on board, because it involves, as we found out, a lot of physical effort, vulnerability, exposure, and plenty else'. They had to weigh these demands against the fact that they were well and happily situated where they were.
>
> 'I didn't know whether I wanted to go through that or not,' she remembers. 'I did not want to be just the General's wife. I had no aspirations for that.'
>
> So how does one deal with such a prospect? 'We had to pray until

we were willing to let the world march through our souls' is Kay's answer.

At the end of their day of prayer had they reached that point?

Paul: 'Yes, we had.'

Kay: 'More or less.'

Paul: 'Oh, I think we had. We said we had. We went forward from there. I left soon after for the High Council [at which he was elected General].'[5]

General John Gowans, elected by the 1999 High Council, reflected on his thoughts and feelings about being nominated in his autobiography *There's a Boy Here*. He writes:

> I was privileged to attend three High Councils and to be nominated each time. This meant a kind of trilogy of testing, if not torture! Three times I had to decide whether or not I should accept nomination, and three times I accepted. Was this the worst kind of vanity on my part? No, it was naïve obedience; I have never refused an appointment.
>
> It was not that I thought I might be chosen for office by my peers, but I did know that God often chooses the weak for his purposes. If he wanted to make such a choice, I should not deprive him of the possibility. I did not propose myself. I could not appoint myself. In an odd way, I felt safe each time and at peace.[6]

As I myself was the Chief of the Staff at the time of the 2002 High Council, I was not unmindful of the fact that I might be nominated to be a candidate for the generalship. My wife Freda and I had thought and prayed about it and had determined what our response would be if it happened. I write in my autobiography: 'We both felt that the doctrine of availability had to be operative. If asked, we would respond that we were available.'[7] It would be yet another instance of *Saying Yes to Life*, as I entitled my memoirs. This was not a time to start saying no.

Following his election as the international leader in 2006, General Shaw Clifton was reminded in an interview that he had been nominated at three High Councils and was asked to tell 'how easy or difficult it is to accept nomination'. He responded:

> Once the nominations are made, the High Council will adjourn…and you will have a sensible length of time to go away and be alone and pray that through.
>
> The first time it happened to me, Helen wasn't there, and I had to call her in Pakistan from London. I was quite taken aback to be nominated. I was only 53 years of age. I was a colonel, which sounds like a high rank, but relative to others in the High Council I was one of the most junior people…
>
> So I was quite surprised to be nominated, but decided I should accept because I just felt this was part of my commitment as an officer. I saw a likeness, a parallel, I suppose, to not declining an appointment as an officer, and just being at God's disposal in the Army…I therefore felt I should accept.
>
> That also gives you an opportunity to address the High Council and gives you an opportunity to answer the many questions, and therefore an opportunity to influence the Army's international agenda. It is a unique chance.
>
> The second time I felt pretty much the same as that. I was only 56 and did not expect to be elected, but felt that the High Council should be honoured by giving it a choice.
>
> Now this most recent time was the hardest of all, and I really was very, very uncertain about it. I didn't really hesitate the first and second time, but this time I was not sure at all. Helen and I drew apart and we were four or five hours agonising about it, praying about it.
>
> Towards the end of that period we got a very clear sense that we should not say no, and I found myself telling the High Council that it was with some reluctance that I accepted nomination. So, to be honest, that did represent a shift in me from the previous occasions. I think the older you get the wiser you get in leadership with an ecclesial body like The Salvation Army. You come to see more clearly what is at stake, and you also have an ever-growing sense of your own lack of worth.[8]

The human drama of saying 'No'

What about those who after reflection choose to say no? It is not uncommon for this to happen. To instance again the 2002 High Council at which I was elected: nine of us were nominated but six chose to decline, leaving only three of us as candidates. Apparently a number of Salvationists who were observing that High Council asked how it could be that so many declined. Are not officers supposed to say yes to appointments?

There is as much human drama in the stories of those who choose to say no as there is in the stories of those who choose to say yes. Those who decline nomination follow in a long tradition. Even at the first High Council in 1929, seven members were nominated but only two accepted. From that High Council onwards it has been fully understood that it is entirely in order and perfectly acceptable for a nominee to decline – and that no explanation is either required or expected. A nomination is not an appointment – it is but an exploratory part of the process of spiritual discernment, and it is right that the person concerned should be part of that process. He or she also has insights to add to the process. Furthermore, given that the default setting for officers is to say yes to each new demand, it is right that nominees should be able to say no without any feeling of guilt.

Nominees who decline nomination do so for a variety of reasons. For some it will be health – their own or that of their spouse – or it might be the age factor or some other personal or family circumstance. Some may feel that however well intentioned the nomination, they are not really cut out for the task. Some may choose to stand aside for a nominee they feel to be more qualified – someone they feel whose time has come. Others, after consulting with the President about the number of nominations they have received, may decide that, as there is little prospect of their being elected, there is little point in subjecting themselves to the demanding process of standing for election. For some the decision will make itself. For others it will be a difficult choice. Some have declined at one High Council and accepted at the next. For each of the nominees there will be the weighing of many factors before clarity is reached in heart and mind.

The responses

When the President of the High Council calls on the nominees in turn to say whether they accept nomination or not, all that they are required to say is either yes or no. However, most nominees choose to clothe their response in a carefully chosen phrase or two or even a longer response. If a nominee is married, his or her spouse speaks to confirm agreement with the decision. The members of the High Council listen attentively and take note.

The President then formally declares that those who have accepted nomination are candidates for the office of General. The Council now has before it a panel of candidates from which the choice of the next General has to be made. Sometimes the panel has been large, as in 1946 when there were eight candidates, or as in 2011 when there were nine. Sometimes the choice has been small, as in 1929, 1969 and 1977 when there were just two candidates.

Action

At this stage of the High Council there is a flurry of activity. The Council is about to embark on a major adjournment – 'at least one full day' state the *Orders of Procedure* – to enable the candidates to prepare written answers to the questions that have been addressed to them and to prepare their speeches. Before that there are a number of things that need to happen.

Fortunately, the fact that spouses of colonel territorial commanders are now present at High Councils means that one previous action demanded at this point has been eliminated. With both spouses of married commissioner couples being present from the 1999 High Council on, the High Council of that year introduced a new order of procedure whereby 'if the spouse of a candidate is not present at the High Council, he or she shall be invited to attend, the Council adjourning until his or her arrival, provided that such invitation shall not be issued if, in the High Council's judgement, substantial delay to the proceedings might be caused thereby'.

The insertion of the new clause in 1999 was providential, for at that High Council two colonels were nominated and accepted nomination: Colonel Shaw Clifton and Colonel Israel L. Gaither. As a result, Colonel Helen Clifton joined the High Council from Pakistan and Colonel Eva D. Gaither from South Africa without there being any significant delay to the process of the Council. They participated in the deliberations of the Council from that point on, but, not being actual members of the Council, they did not vote.

That is now all history, but in the same spirit, should in future a married person from outside the High Council be nominated and accept nomination, the *Orders of Procedure* state that the invitation to attend the High Council will include the spouse.

Action points

But the following points need action by the High Council before it adjourns:

Firstly, a news release giving the names of the nominees and candidates has to be issued. The High Council communications officer, who has been writing regular bulletins describing the process and 'atmosphere' of the High Council, now at last has some hard news to share.

Successive High Councils have taken different views as to whether just the names of those who have accepted nomination should be released or whether the full list of nominees, including any declining nominees, should be made known. The question has been discussed as the High Councils have determined their *Orders of Procedure*. Some members have felt that what is most important is that no nominee who has withdrawn should be embarrassed. Others have felt that it is important and right that the Salvationist family should know the names of all who have been nominated. They have argued that few if any declining nominees would be embarrassed by the disclosure of their names, and that, on the contrary, they should consider their nomination to be a badge of honour.

The early High Councils had no ruling on the matter, but the 1954 High Council added to its *Orders of Procedure* that only the names of those accepting nomination would be disclosed to the media. That policy remained in force until 1999. The High Council of that year, after debate, broke that tradition and settled for a middle position. Since then the policy has been that the names of *all* nominees are released 'except for the names and other identifying details of any declining nominees who request non-publication'. However, the names of declining nominees at some of the earlier High Councils that were not announced at the time of the High Council have since appeared in the official history of The Salvation Army.[9]

Secondly, the service records of the candidates are made available to members as part of the 'getting to know you' process. These documents are again purely factual and contain no value judgements.

Thirdly, any High Council office holders who have become candidates or are spouses of candidates have at this point to step down from their tasks, and replacements have to be elected or appointed. A number of High Council Presidents have been nominated but thus far only two Presidents have accepted nomination and become candidates. The first was Commissioner Clarence Wiseman at the 1974 High Council. In that instance, the Vice-President, Commissioner Francis Evans, took over as President. Commissioner Wiseman went on to become the General-elect. The second President to become a candidate was Commissioner William W. Francis in 2011. He was succeeded as President by Commissioner James M. Knaggs.

Fourthly, the approved questionnaire for candidates and, if married, the questionnaire for spouses have to be formally presented to the people concerned. Now that the identity of the candidates is known, opportunity has also to be given for members to submit questions addressed to individual candidates. Such questions have to be approved by the Questions Committee and by the High Council as a whole, a process which has to be completed before the Council can adjourn.

When these various matters have been attended to, the President announces the day and time when the High Council will meet again and then declares the proceedings adjourned.

With the members having spent many days together in intensive conference the prospect of a break comes as welcome relief with opportunity for relaxation, catching up with emails and for seasons of prayer. The happy chatter of members as they leave the hall tells its own story.

For the candidates, however, the day ahead is going to be one of intense concentration and hard work.

Chapter Seven
Questions

AS the sun rises on a new day the candidates and their spouses are already hard at work in their rooms grappling with their responses to the questionnaires. Like so many other aspects of the High Council the process of addressing questions to the candidates has its own history of development.

To question or not to question?

No questions were addressed to the candidates at the first High Council in 1929. The two candidates simply made a speech after which the Council proceeded to the actual election.

When the first purely electoral High Council was held in 1934 the issue arose as to whether it was permissible and right for the Council to address questions to the candidates. Following discussion the Council resolved 'that members of the Council may, by means of a questionnaire, ask the candidates questions relating to the duties of the General and the work of the Army, such questionnaire to be prepared and approved by a committee of seven members of the Council'. Seven members were duly elected and the Questions Committee was formed.

Despite this step it seems that the Council was still unsure as to whether it had the right under the 1904 Supplementary Deed of Constitution to address questions to candidates or even to require them to give a speech. Attention was drawn to the clause in the deed which stated that the High Council 'shall immediately after the constitution thereof...proceed to the election of a General'. The Council therefore decided to ask its legal adviser for his counsel on the point.

Mr William Frost attended the next day and explained that the word 'immediately' referred to the beginning of a process, and not to its conclusion, and that the High Council had full control of what the process itself should or should not include. The 'immediately', he explained, was like the guard of the Scotland Express calling the passengers to board the train in London without delay but the journey would not be complete until the train arrived in Edinburgh. The High Council had already begun its journey – Mr Frost reckoned it had reached York by now – and had full freedom to decide what that journey should include before it arrived at its destination.

However, even with the reassurances from Mr Frost, the Council remained uncertain as to whether it was appropriate for it to restrict the freedom of action of the next General by requiring him or her to answer questions as a candidate. The Council therefore, after 'considerable discussion and various amendments', decided to reverse its original decision. It resolved to 'rescind the resolution providing for a questionnaire to be submitted to the candidates; and that the election be proceeded without questions, but that the candidates may, if they so desire, make speeches on agreeing to nomination.'

By the next High Council, in 1939, the climate of thinking had changed. In preparation for the Council, Mr Frost was asked to prepare constitutional notes by way of answers to a series of questions asked of him. A key question, as already noted, was whether the journey the High Council was taking could include stops for discussion of issues affecting the Army. To this Mr Frost had given a robust affirmative by stating that 'the High Council is supreme in regulating its own procedure and thus saying what shall or shall not be discussed and in what manner the discussion shall take place'.[1] The document continued:

> **Question**: Is it proper to ask a candidate what are his views and intentions in relation to any of these issues (or any other Salvation Army issues) in the event of his being appointed [by election]?

Answer: Yes, if the High Council so desires. How else are you to ascertain who is the most suitable person to be appointed? It is not only your privilege but your duty to thresh out these issues to the uttermost before you cast your vote. This is the highest duty that you owe to The Salvation Army in whose interest and for whose future welfare and safety the vote is given to you.

Question: Is it proper and permissible to ask a candidate to give promises or pledges upon any of these issues?

Answer: Yes, if the High Council so desires. But promises or pledges thus given have only an honourable and moral value. They cannot be transmuted into legal conditions of appointment. There can be no conditional appointment – only an absolutely unconditional one. If a General, after appointment, were to dishonour his pledges, a future High Council could be summoned to depose him, but in the meantime his appointment would stand and his authority would be absolute. As the possibility of such dishonour is happily remote, such pledges would therefore have a definite value, and it would be legitimate for a voter to ask any candidate for a pledge he thought valuable to the Army and to let the giving or refusing of it weigh with him in his judgement of that candidate.

There was no hesitation on the part of Mr Frost in asserting the right of a High Council to ask questions and even to exact pledges from candidates, and succeeding High Councils have followed the guidance given. But though pledges have sometimes been asked of candidates on specific points, the asking of questions has never been in the nature of adversarial exchanges. On the contrary, the question period has been seen as part of the spiritual exercise of discernment.

High Council members are experienced leaders and recognise that candidates do not have full knowledge of every situation they may face if elected as General. They also know that constitutionally the High Council as a body cannot fetter the right and duty of the future General to act in any matter as he or she thinks best for the

Army in the light of fuller knowledge and changing circumstances. They further understand that it would be unreasonable to expect a candidate in a matter of a few hours to prepare and present a fully worked out plan for his or her generalship. Answers on intended policy – as contrasted to commitments on specific points – are therefore seen more as statements of intent in the light of present knowledge than as firm pledges.

The candidates themselves are of course also experienced leaders and understand how inadvisable it is for them to give firm promises on issues of which they may not yet have complete knowledge. General Wilfred Kitching comments about his own responses at the High Council which elected him: 'I was not unconscious of the fact that there are some questions which at best can be answered only by a promise to give, if elected, subsequent consideration to the issue raised. Before one can make a final commitment there are some questions upon which one must seek advice no matter how urgent the issue may appear to be at first sight. The hands of a candidate should never be tied, and I have always had the greatest respect for those who have refused to accept a proposal, knowing that their answer might jeopardise their election.'[2]

General Frederick Coutts endorses this approach, writing that the questions enable High Council members to express their concerns, but that 'the wise nominee will not deliver himself bound hand and foot to a particular solution. Not until he sits down in his office at "101" and calls for the file will he know the truth, the whole truth, and nothing but the truth on some contentious point…To announce a line of action in advance is to make an error of judgment. After all, no member of a High Council knows all the facts for none has ever sat in the General's chair.'[3]

Though there is no legal obligation on a General to act in accordance with answers given to questions at the High Council during his or her term of office, Generals have nevertheless felt a moral commitment to do so. Where fuller knowledge or changed circumstances have made it necessary for them to take a different course of action on some matter than the one they anticipated taking when responding at the High Council, such action has been preceded by consultation and accompanied by an explanation.

Some Generals, at a later stage of their term of office, have chosen to render account of their stewardship with respect to answers given at the High Council, either through a written document circulated to all who were members of the Council or as a presentation to a subsequent meeting of the General's Consultative Council.

The Questions Committee

As established already in 1934, the preparation of the questions for candidates is entrusted to an elected Questions Committee of seven members. This committee is given the responsibility of supervising the compilation of three separate questionnaires. First, the General Questionnaire with questions addressed to all the candidates. Second, on the rare occasions when it arises, any individually addressed questions to specific candidates by name. And third, since 1999, a Spouse Questionnaire with questions addressed to the spouses of candidates.

As previously noted, the seven members of the committee are elected as early as possible in a meeting of the High Council. This enables them to prepare the questionnaires and get them approved by the Council while the Council is still in the procedural stage of its deliberations, that is, before nominations are made and the candidates are identified.[4]

Preparation of the General Questionnaire

Every member of a High Council has the right to submit a question for the General Questionnaire. Questions have to be signed – no anonymous questions are accepted – and are handed to the President. The President in turn passes the questions on to the Questions Committee – but without the signature of the questioner, so that it is only the President who knows the authorship of each question.

Until the 1990s great weight was given to the right of each Council member not only to ask one or more questions, but also to have his or her question included in the questionnaire unless the questioner agreed to its omission. As earlier *Orders of Procedure* put it: 'No question may be altered in its intention or rejected by the committee without the concurrence of the questioner. In case of failure to agree on any point it shall be referred to the full Council.'

The task of the Questions Committee in earlier High Councils was therefore to eliminate duplicates, conflate similar questions into one, and suggest to questioners when necessary that their question be omitted. This procedure tended to result in a General Questionnaire of around 24 questions. So as not to have to start from scratch each time, High Councils have usually had sight of the questionnaire prepared by the previous High Council. General Wilfred Kitching recalls that at the 1954 High Council 'the 24 questions submitted on this occasion did not greatly differ from those given to candidates in the 1946 High Council'.[5]

However, with the passage of time an inflationary process set in, and by 1981, as General Jarl Wahlström recalls, 'the questions submitted in writing were combined in a questionnaire with more than 30 main headings. When the sub headings were included, there were more than 100 questions about different subjects.'[6]

By 1993 this spurt of creativity led the 50 members of the High Council to submit no less than 240 unduplicated questions! It was clear that it had become impossible to honour even the intention of trying to include all questions. The *Orders of Procedure* on the submission of questions were therefore suspended, members were asked to indicate which questions they considered most important, and with this guidance the Questions Committee produced a General Questionnaire of just 40 questions which was approved by the Council as a whole.

In the light of that experience the 1994 High Council adopted new procedures for the compilation of the General Questionnaire. These revised procedures, which have been accepted by all High Councils since then, seek to find an appropriate balance between the rights of members to submit questions and the rights of the Council as a whole.

By these revised procedures the Questions Committee is requested to supervise the production of a General Questionnaire of not more than 40 questions, and is asked to begin the process by preparing the draft of up to 18 standard questions that will form the heart of the questionnaire. This draft is then circulated to all members of the Council and members are invited to submit any further questions they might have, but are limited to one question each. If questions have been prepared by the Council as a body following discussions in the Committee of the Whole, these are also added. The Questions Committee then prepares 'the final draft of the General Questionnaire, exercising its judgment in the selection of questions submitted in order to arrive at a balanced General Questionnaire of the prescribed length'. The finished draft is finally reviewed by the High Council as a whole, amended if necessary, and then approved.

Content of the General Questionnaire

To review the questions in the General Questionnaires since 1939 is to review the history of the internal and external issues uppermost in the minds of members at the time of each Council.

In the early High Councils the questions centred on constitutional issues, adherence to the Army's doctrines, equal opportunities for women and men, promotion of the Army's internationalism, with shades of the constitutional turbulence of 1929 showing through with questions like:

> Will you agree not to give preferential treatment in the matters of promotion, class of appointment, and advancement of position to any members of your family or other relatives who now are or may be in the future officers of The Salvation Army?

> Will you promise not to appoint your wife, or the wife of any other active officer, to a position with the rank of commissioner, or lieut-

commissioner in her own right, thus making her eligible for membership of the High Council?

Are you willing to give a pledge that you will retire in harmony with the existing regulation governing the retirement of the General?

As will be recalled, in 1946 the matter of an Advisory Council to the General was the hot issue of the day. Following the three days spent discussing the issue as a Committee of the Whole, the Council as a body prepared the following question:

> In view of the overwhelming expression of the 1946 High Council, will you, if elected General, constitute and throughout your term of office maintain, an Advisory Council for the purpose of study, research and exploration and to advise you on matters of importance on which you may require advice or counsel; and, further in order to bring this Council into being, will you immediately upon assuming office appoint a commission of five commissioners, two of whom shall be from overseas, to study the various Advisory Council functional plans which have been or may be submitted by the international commissioners and the territorial commanders, this commission to submit its report to you within six months, the report as approved by you to be sent without delay to the international commissioners and the territorial commanders to the end that the permanent Advisory Council shall be appointed and functioning within one year of the date of your assumption of office?

In the 1950s and 60s, High Councils sought assurances that the Advisory Council to the General would be maintained and that specified matters would be referred to it. The scope of the questionnaire also gradually widened to include questions on the various aspects of the Army's mission, such as missionary work, evangelism, social services, training and youth.

As the Army advanced into the 1970s and 80s, issues added to the questionnaire included finance, the worldwide expansion of the

Army, the relationship with the World Council of Churches, the charismatic movement, the role of the General in the administration of the Army in Britain, and the Army's response to the scourge of HIV/Aids.

The end of the 20th century and the commencement of the 21st brought their own crop of questions on specific issues of the day such as homosexuality and the Army's stance on the sacraments. A question that has always been included is about the candidate's health, past and present.

With the passage of time the *style* of question addressed to candidates has changed. In the earlier High Councils most questions could be answered with a yes or a no, or with a sentence or two at the most. But as the High Council process has evolved, the questions have increasingly been seen as a key component of the 'getting to know you' process. This in turn has had the effect of changing the style of the questions so as to require longer, essay-style answers designed to explore at greater depth the candidate's thinking and personality. In fact, such has been the development of this type of question that recent High Councils have not felt it necessary to make use of the full quota of 40 questions permitted by the *Orders of Procedure*.

An overview of the content of contemporary General Questionnaires can be gained by the headings under which questions have been grouped. In recent High Councils these have sometimes been brief – Personal, Mission, Governance, Vision – and sometimes longer:

- Spiritual leadership
- Vision
- Mission
- Belief and practice
- Personnel
- Governance and strategy.

The following sample questions needing more discursive replies give the flavour of a modern-day questionnaire:

Describe your leadership style. How would becoming the General impact this style?

Describe your vision for The Salvation Army. What mission priorities could contribute to achieving this vision?

Identify and describe the relevance of Salvation Army distinctives in today's world.

What do you see as the key considerations in safeguarding The Salvation Army as a unified, diverse and international movement?

Follow-up questions

As a result of a recommendation made by the 1995 Commission on the High Council, accepted by the 1999 High Council and all subsequent High Councils, after each candidate has read out his or her answers to the General Questionnaire there follows a 10-minute period for follow-up questions. During this time members of the Council can, through the President, seek clarification about any of the responses given.

The President ensures that all follow-up questions do relate to a response already made by the candidate and that they do not subtly introduce new questions – perhaps for which there was no space in the General Questionnaire.

Individually addressed questions

Once the names of the candidates are known it also becomes possible for members of the High Council to address personal questions to individual candidates. An individually addressed question has to do with the circumstances and personal history of the candidate addressed and by definition cannot be answered by any other candidate. 'What are your views on euthanasia?' would not pass the test as an individually addressed question, for the question could be addressed to any of the candidates. The question must relate to the addressed candidate alone.

An example of an individually addressed question is the question addressed to Commissioner Frederick Coutts at the 1963 High Council. He tells in his autobiography that he was asked about the prospect of his wife recovering her health following the loss of the use of her legs as a result of a routine vaccination.[7] In other instances candidates have been asked about specific events in their past service.

Looking ahead, when in the future there may well be a married woman among the candidates, it is likely that by means of an individually addressed question she will be asked how she sees the role of her husband if she is elected General. The High Council might even wish to explore the same subject directly with her husband by means of an individually addressed question. If so, the *Orders of Procedure* would need to be amended to permit an individually addressed question to a spouse.

As already indicated, individually addressed questions are not often asked at High Councils, but provision for such questions exists in the *Orders of Procedure*.

Spouse questionnaire

Not until the 1999 High Council were the spouses of married candidates present at the High Council. Reference has been made earlier to the problem of High Council members not knowing the candidates well, but the candidates were at least present at the Council and members could form their own judgement. However, when it came to the *wife* of a candidate, the only information members had was what the candidate said in reply to the questions about his wife. Many High Council members in the past have cast their votes and elected a General without ever having seen or met his wife.

Until the 1999 High Council the General Questionnaire had usually included one or more questions for a married candidate about his wife, on the following lines: Was she willing to share with her husband the demands of international leadership? Had she taken an active part in platform and other ministry through the years? What role did the candidate see her taking in the future?

Now that the spouses of candidates would be present, the 1999 High Council had to decide to what degree, if any, the spouses of candidates should be formally scrutinised by the High Council. The 1995 Commission on the High Council had grappled with this issue and was sensitive to two complementary facts: first, that the High Council exists to elect a General, not a couple; second, that the role of the spouse in the Army setting is uniquely vital. With the new and positive development that the spouse would be present at the High Council, what had to be determined was the procedure that would most sensitively balance these two contrasting factors.

It was clear that it would be intolerable for the candidate to answer questions about his or her spouse now that the spouse would be present. The 1995 Commission on the High Council therefore recommended, and the 1999 High Council accepted, that the spouse should be required to answer a short questionnaire of up to six questions, but would not be asked to give a speech. This has remained the standard pattern.

The questions addressed to spouses have mainly been of the 'getting to know you' type – including health – and at recent High Councils have been carefully designed to be appropriate for either a male or female spouse. Following are some typical examples of questions that have been included in the spouse questionnaire:

> What personal qualities do you possess and how do they complement your spouse's ministry?
>
> How would you view your ministry at International Headquarters and throughout the world as the spouse of the General?
>
> How do you feel God has used your leadership to advance his mission?

The preparation of answers

In earlier High Councils no time was scheduled for candidates to prepare their answers to questions or to draft their speeches. It was not unusual for the nominees to accept nomination and become candidates towards the end of one working day, and for the President then to announce that the Council would meet at the usual time the next morning to hear the candidates' answers and their speeches. This meant that the candidates often had to work through the night. And in the days of secretaries and shorthand dictation, relays of secretaries were on hand to take dictation from the candidates and to type up the full documents as they emerged, so that everything was ready by the morning.

The 1995 Commission on the High Council felt that this was asking too much of the candidates and was neither good for them personally nor for the High Council in its function of discernment. If in preparing answers to questions candidates devoted only an average of 12 minutes to each question, with a questionnaire of 40 questions that would add up to eight hours of intense mental work. The Commission therefore recommended that the High Council should adjourn 'for at least one full day to enable candidates to prepare answers to the questionnaires and also their speeches'. This proposal was accepted by the 1999 High Council and has remained the procedure ever since.

These days candidates tend to work on their laptops with a steady stream of answers in electronic form flowing to the secretariat for processing during the day, whether as attachments to emails or by use of USB flash drives or compact discs.

Presentation of responses

When the High Council reconvenes after the day-long adjournment all candidates and spouses come armed with a document that sets out their answers to the questions in the questionnaires. Copies of this document will be made available to all members of the High Council when each candidate responds. Candidates are required to keep to their written scripts and, in the interest of fairness, are not permitted to ad-lib in the light of further inspiration or as prompted by the response of some other candidate. To further ensure absolute fairness between the candidates, the order in which they respond to the questions is determined by ballot.

The President calls the first candidate to the podium and asks for copies of the relevant paper, containing both the questions and answers, to be distributed to all members. The candidate reads his or her responses while the members listen intently in silence and follow with their eyes the written script. Then follows the opportunity for follow-up questions. If the candidate is married, his or her spouse after this responds to the questions in the Spouse Questionnaire.

The process demands concentration not only on the part of the speaker but also from the listeners. In recent High Councils this process has taken on average around one hour per candidate. In 2011, when there were nine candidates, that will have meant nine hours or more of concentrated listening for the members of the Council.

The members of the High Council listen not only to what is being said, but also to what is not being said. They read not only the lines before them but also read 'between the lines'. They observe how candidates handle difficult questions; they note the convictions that come through, the commitments that are made, the judgement that is shown. They watch the candidates' demeanour under pressure and appreciate a lighter touch where this is appropriate. As they listen they gradually form an impression of the potential each candidate has for the office of General. The impression may reinforce what they already feel or may change their thinking about the potential of the person speaking.

Following the hours devoted to questions and answers, the members of the High Council are left with much to ponder – and time is set aside for that. When the information gained from the question-and-answer session has been absorbed, the High Council moves on to the next stage: the candidates' speeches.

The smallest High Council to date.
The 1974 High Council with 40 members which elected General Clarence Wiseman.

The purpose-built High Council conference suite at Sunbury Court, Sunbury-on-Thames, near London, UK.

The largest High Council to date.
The 2013 High Council with 117 members which elected General André Cox.

Generals elected by a High Council

General Edward Higgins
Elected 1929

General Evangeline Booth
Elected 1934

General George Carpenter
Elected 1939

General Albert Orsborn
Elected 1946

General Wilfred Kitching
Elected 1954

General Frederick Coutts
Elected 1963

General Erik Wickberg
Elected 1969

General Clarence Wiseman
Elected 1974

General Arnold Brown
Elected 1977

General Jarl Wahlström
Elected 1981

General Eva Burrows
Elected 1986

General Bramwell Tillsley
Elected 1993

General Paul A. Rader
Elected 1994

General John Gowans
Elected 1999

General John Larsson
Elected 2002

General Shaw Clifton
Elected 2006

General Linda Bond
Elected 2011

General André Cox
Elected 2013

Chapter Eight

Speeches

THE speeches which the candidates give are their only opportunity to lay before the High Council, in a formal way, their thoughts about the generalship and their vision for the future. The speeches are therefore a vital part of the process and it is only natural that the candidates give much thought to what they are going to say – and how they are going to say it. The speech must strike the right note and be the right length. Its delivery can also pose a challenge. Candidates have to speak from a prepared script, which members will have before them during the speech, whereas most of them would normally speak in a freer style from notes. The challenge is therefore how to sound like themselves despite this limitation.

The speeches can prove decisive. At the 1929 High Council there were two candidates, Commissioner Edward Higgins, the Chief of the Staff, and Commander Evangeline Booth, the USA National Commander. Because of the special circumstances of that High Council the delegates had already been together for 37 days when it came to speech time and had participated in many discussions. Yet Commissioner Samuel Brengle, who was a member of that High Council, reckoned that it was the speeches that decided the outcome of the election. He recalled that 'the councillors compared the Commander's speech with the speech by Commissioner Higgins and many of them, I think, there and then finally decided for Higgins. One most prominent commissioner told me that he was undecided until he heard the two speeches.'[1]

The *Orders of Procedure* establish that the order in which the candidates are to speak is determined by ballot, and that after each speech there will be a five-minute period for silent reflection before the next candidate speaks.

To speak or not to speak?

At the 1929 High Council the two candidates were 'invited' to speak, and both accepted. When more formal orders of procedure were established at the next High Council, in 1934, it was stated that 'nominees may, if they so desire, make speeches on agreeing to nomination'. This voluntary approach to speech-making was institutionalised in the *Orders of Procedure* of the 1939 High Council – which also laid down guidelines for the listeners:

> That each nominee may make one speech only, if he or she desires; that the speeches be heard without interruption of any kind; and that at the conclusion there be no expression either of approval or dissent.

This perfectly understandable rule about listeners not reacting overtly brings its own challenge to both speakers and hearers. Army speakers are used to getting some kind of response from the congregation – and total silence can be disconcerting. From the point of view of the hearers, it may be self-evident that it is not appropriate to exclaim 'hallelujah!' or even 'amen' to express agreement with something said, but not so self-evident whether they can laugh if the speaker says something humorous. Most do.

The voluntary basis of speeches remained in the *Orders of Procedure* for the first six High Councils – but all candidates invariably chose to address the Council and that pattern became accepted as the norm.

However, at the 1969 High Council, when the two candidates were Commissioner Erik Wickberg and Commissioner Kaare Westergaard, that norm was challenged. General Erik Wickberg describes in his autobiography what happened:

> For the first time in High Council history the two candidates did not give a speech, where they are expected to present their views on how

they see themselves discharging the duties of General if elected.

I had discovered that the *Orders of Procedure* prescribed that a candidate 'could' give such a speech, but that he clearly could choose whether or not to use this opportunity. As I had answered in great detail the more than 30 written questions that had been put to me and to Westergaard, I did not think there was much more to add.

The President of the High Council, Commissioner Hubert Scotney, approved my interpretation of that paragraph, and as Westergaard agreed with my viewpoint there were no speeches.[2]

Commissioner Erik Wickberg was correct in his reading of the rules, and had every right not to speak to the High Council. What is perhaps surprising is that he sought – successfully, as it turned out – to persuade Commissioner Kaare Westergaard to join with him in not giving a speech. In 1969 Commissioner Wickberg had been the Chief of the Staff for nine years, serving under both General Wilfred Kitching and General Frederick Coutts, and was therefore well known to every member of the High Council. Commissioner Westergaard was less well known and the opportunity to address the Council could have been valuable to his candidacy.

Commissioner Westergaard later regretted that he had not taken hold of the chance to speak to the Council in order to lay before it his own thinking about the generalship. It appears that his regret was shared by others, for at the next High Council, held in 1974, the rules were changed and the voluntary element in the making of speeches was removed from the *Orders of Procedure*. In 1974 it became, and remains, a requirement that candidates address the Council.

Length of speeches

The *Orders of Procedure* give no guidance regarding content or even length of the speeches. This is left entirely to the discretion of the candidates, and the speeches at successive High Councils reveal great variations in both content and length.

The longest speech was given by Commander Evangeline Booth

at the 1929 High Council when she spoke for 53 minutes. The 1929 High Council was of course unique and there were many issues that had to be covered, especially as there was no opportunity for questions at that Council. The record for the shortest speech is held jointly by two American officers – Commissioner Norman Marshall in 1954 and Commissioner Kenneth L. Hodder in 1994 – who each spoke for four minutes.

The length of speeches given by candidates who subsequently were elected as General have ranged from eight minutes (Commissioner John Gowans) to 31 minutes (Commissioner Albert Orsborn), with the average length being 16 minutes. For those interested in statistical minutiae, the lengths of the speeches by candidates who were elected General are listed in an endnote.[3]

Content of speeches

It is of interest to get the flavour of speeches given by candidates at High Councils. In the earlier Councils no records were kept of the text of the speeches, but there are references in memoirs and biographies. In more recent times a number of Generals have published their nomination speeches in full. What follows is a brief selection from these sources.

At the 1939 High Council, the self-effacing Commissioner George Carpenter made no secret of the fact that he felt that someone else should become the General. From correspondence we know that the person he had in mind was Lieut-Commissioner Albert Orsborn. In the biography of her father, Stella Carpenter writes: 'Commissioner Carpenter spoke for 11 minutes, and the President admonished him – not without a dash of humour – that he was speaking for himself and not on behalf of a younger man. "I did not do well" says his diary.'[4]

Of the 1954 High Council, General Wilfred Kitching recalls in his autobiography that 'the morning of May 11th dawned with a heavy sense of responsibility resting upon all, occasioned by awe rather than by fear. I read the notes of what I felt led to say to the Council in my election speech. Some sentences I felt to be unnecessary and

I saw the danger of saying more than was needed…It was not for me to say what a General should be or not be, and it was equally unwise to make too many promises as to what I would do if elected. In that early morning hour I wrote at the head of my notes words Paul had written to the Corinthians: "For not he that commendeth himself is approved, but whom the Lord commendeth." And that I felt was the best and first thing to be said.'[5]

Commissioner Frederick Coutts began his speech at the 1963 High Council by saying: 'I would apply to the office of a General a saying of John Quincy Adams concerning the Presidency of the United States – that it is an office neither to be solicited nor to be declined. I have not done the former, and happily the decision on the latter rests with the High Council.'

He then spoke about his three aims if elected. 'The first would be to confirm the faith of the Army in its divine mission…In the second place, to confirm the faith of the Army in its place and function in the church universal …' On this subject he said:

> We must spell this out for our people – particularly our young people – so that they may understand that they have no need to seek elsewhere for the essential grace which can be found within our own walls, nor can any churchly blessing make them more truly members of the heavenly kingdom than they are by faith in Jesus as Saviour and Lord. And spell it out for our officers as well so that nowhere will any of them – woman or man, single or married – be received as any other than a minister of the gospel, 'as poor, yet making many rich; as having nothing, and yet possessing all things.'

'In the third place,' he continued, 'to confirm the faith of the Army in the integrity of its own government. This calls for informed leadership…especially when, as with our structure, a General is both the source of authority and the final court of appeal. This means that he must be free from the very appearance of partiality, and never allow any domestic conversation to interfere with, much less take the place of, the counsel of his appointed officers…'[6]

General Arnold Brown published in full his speech at the 1977 High Council as an appendix to his autobiography. He outlined what he saw as the General's task in a series of numbered points which he then expanded upon:

> 1. The General's lead must, above all, be spiritual. 2. He must call Salvationists to a renewed emphasis upon our doctrine. 3. He must see to it that wherever and whenever possible administration will be streamlined. 4. He must be a General for youth. 5. He must ensure the enlargement of 'the female ministry'. 6. He must speed the progress of the Army in the developing countries. 7. He must increase the place of our soldiery. 8. He must arouse Salvationists to the desperate need for officer reinforcements. 9. He must be committed to the principle of *one* Salvation Army – not a federation of autonomous Salvation Armies.[7]

General Jarl Wahlström in his memoirs mentions how at the 1981 High Council he took spiritual leadership as the theme for his speech. 'Leadership in the Army must first and foremost be spiritual leadership...A spiritual leader must have inner balance, and it is important that his leadership is equally balanced...There must be an adequate balance between the desk and the pulpit...A Salvation Army leader must promote the balance between the Army's evangelical and social work...Further, he must strike a balance between sound conservatism and courageous new thinking...A spiritual leader must be prepared to ask for and listen to advice from experienced and knowledgeable members of his team, and from others...A spiritual leader must be a person with clear principles and at the same time a warm heart...General Bramwell Booth spoke of Army officers as "servants of all". The one elected to be their leader must be "the servant of the servants".'[8]

The way that General Eva Burrows approached the task of giving a speech at the 1986 High Council is described by Henry Gariepy, her biographer:

> Nominees were also asked to prepare their views on the role of the General, to be given the following day. Working late into the night on the topic of leadership, Eva became uneasy. She prayed about her speech. Even though the hour was late, she felt led to scrap what she had been preparing and start over, this time on the leadership of Jesus. Once she came to this concept her thoughts flowed. The next day she spoke on how she would want to pattern her leadership style after that of Jesus.[9]

Commissioner Bramwell Tillsley began his speech at the 1993 High Council by saying: 'Perhaps I can best express what my own priorities would be by describing the Army for which I long'. After affirming his personal commitment to the statement in the Officer's Covenant 'I will live to win souls', he spoke about his longings for the Army under a series of headings:

> I long for an Army whose motto is 'holiness unto the Lord'...I long for an Army open and responsive to the leading of the Holy Spirit...I long for an Army that will serve in the spirit of the Master...I long for an Army that will remain true to its principles, no matter what the cost...I long for an Army that has a deep appreciation of its young people and that encourages them to find their full potential in Christ...I long for an Army committed to prayer and the ministry of the Word...I long for an Army that is international in its outlook and recognises its responsibility to the whole world...I long for an Army whose cardinal reason for existence is to bring glory to God.[10]

At the 1994 High Council Commissioner Paul A. Rader took strategic advance as his theme. 'These times call for a fighting force – furiously aggressive – a militant Army, disciplined to proclaim Jesus as Lord, amid the meanness and misery of our world. These times call for an advancing Army.' He continued:

> We must go forward in finding cost-effective, supportable means for entering new areas of ministry;...forward in compassionate and

creative response to the AIDS pandemic;...forward in our efforts to find and enfold the lost and then enlist them in our great cause;...forward in aggressive and innovative approaches to evangelism;...forward in our efforts to sensitise and mobilise our people to confront the moral crises in our communities;...forward in our commitment as an Army – east and west, north and south – to world evangelisation.

We must advance in a continuing renewal of faith and spiritual vigour...We must move forward together in all our rich cultural diversity...We must share a common strategic vision as we move aggressively toward the 21st century.[11]

In 1999 Commissioner John Gowans began his speech in characteristic style:

Did you ever find yourself in a particular place and get the feeling that you have been there before? This is the third time I have been called upon to make this kind of speech, and the elder statesmen among us may well be wondering why I am presenting myself as a candidate once again. 'Can't the man take no for an answer?' they may well be justified in asking!

I have the temerity to speak to this High Council of my peers simply because, whilst many things have changed since last this Council gathered, two things have not changed: my dedication to God and my availability to his Salvation Army.

I have sometimes been tempted to do so, but I have never refused any appointment which my leaders thought good to entrust to me. In this situation *you* are my leaders. I will do what you tell me.

If you decide under the guidance of God that I am the person to lead The Salvation Army into the 21st century I shall be proud to accept that honour. If you decide that I should quietly prepare for retirement I will accept that honour with equal cheerfulness.[12]

In my own speech to the 2002 High Council I shared with members that one of my chief aims if elected as General would be to encourage the process of renewal which I believed God was inspiring within the Army. 'It seems to me,' I said, 'that in recent years, as the Army has sought to rediscover its roots it is rediscovering its mission.' My aim, I stated, would be to keep the Army continually focused on its three-fold mission of saving souls, growing saints and serving suffering humanity. I continued:

> In this process of renewal I believe we are also recovering the vision of what the Army is meant to be. We are rediscovering the genius of the original vision. That is essential, for in some parts of the world we have been through a time of lack of confidence in ourselves. Everyone has thought us to be wonderful – everyone except ourselves! And there have been – and remain – pressures for us to become pale imitations of other churches and movements. I would aim to encourage the renewal of confidence in the unique contribution that the Army was raised up to make.
>
> The Army is a force, not a flock...It is a force that is visible...A force with a mission to the whole person...A force with a genius for inclusion and releasing of potential...A force with a special mission to the disadvantaged...
>
> I believe that God is powerfully at work in our midst to renew our passion for mission. I believe that he is at work to renew our vision of all that he wants the Army to be in the 21st century. My main focus would be to seek to encourage that process of renewal by every possible means.[13]

At the 2006 High Council Commissioner Shaw Clifton emphasised that Jesus was the centre of his life, and that the strength he sought was 'not any strength that flows from human ability or natural talent' but from reliance 'on real faith upon a God who says that when we are weak, then he is strong'. In speaking about 'the picture of the Army I believe God wants to see,' he said:

> Already we are an Army loved and used by God. He wants us, however, to be closer yet to his side. It is a wounded side. He wants us to be broken again. He wants to break, melt and fill the Army...

He wants us to be a truthful Army, an honest Army, never pretending that all is well, never vaunting ourselves or seeking the plaudits of men...He wants us to be a united, international Army...He wants us to be a spiritual Army...He wants us to be a Christ-centred, Cross-conscious Army...

He wants an Army led by a General who is close to him, who is not transfixed or dazzled by the position, but is ready to spend and to be spent for Christ and the people. He wants a General sound in doctrine, with a heart of compassion, a humane General, someone who will affirm and encourage... He wants a General who will have a crucified mind, a broken and contrite heart, a surrendered intellect, a passion for the things of God.[14]

Commissioner Linda Bond at the 2011 High Council took as her headings: Our World, Our Army, Our Leadership, and Our God. In speaking about her vision for the Army she said:

I see a Spirit-filled Army of the 21st century, convinced of its calling, moving forward together into the world of the hurting, broken, lonely, dispossessed and lost, reaching them by all means with the transforming message of Jesus, bringing freedom, hope and life.

The lengthy discussions about our identity need to come to an end if they haven't already. It is vital that we are convinced of why we exist. When we have such a certainty, this one mission will bring us together as one Army, every nation, every generation; every Salvationist totally sold out to our calling by God.

We were never meant to hide inside the walls of our buildings. We are God's gift to the world...We belong on the front lines, in the gutters, in the dark places of our world. Our people are the marginalised...Transformation for us is more than giving a job to the unemployed, a grocery voucher to the hungry, a bed to the homeless. The transformation that the Army has been known for is the transformation only Jesus can give, salvation for the whole person, body, soul and mind...

It is time to rally our people for life's greatest cause. To be the people we were called to be, to do what we were called to do, to be an Army faithful to the gospel, is to be an Army blessed by God.[15]

At the 2013 High Council Commissioner André Cox addressed the members of the High Council as 'the international leadership team of The Salvation Army' and stressed that 'our people want us to provide leadership that is in accordance with the spiritual values we proclaim'. He then dealt with five specific aspects:

> *Youth Work.* We need to listen to and answer the questions of our young people…They will not build the Army of tomorrow in the way we have built. [But] one day they will take over from us. It is important that they build an Army that is relevant to the world in which they live, remaining faithful to the specific call of God for The Salvation Army.
>
> *Teaching and Preaching.* I would love to see an Army that truly lives by what it preaches. We need to see more evidence of power, conviction and passion in all that we do. Perhaps we need to re-discover the blazing power of the Spirit that swept through our ranks in days gone by.
>
> *Leadership Development.* Still today we see people who are parachuted into appointments with little preparation and they often are left to either sink or swim! We need to be far more systematic in the way that we prepare and bring on the next generation of leaders.
>
> *Financial Security.* We face huge and daunting challenges in both the developed and developing worlds…How can we ensure that all officers receive their full allowance? In some places there are far too many officers in field appointments who are disadvantaged financially compared to their colleagues serving on divisional and territorial headquarters.
>
> *Ethics and Good Governance.* The Salvation Army should be above all reproach in the way that we deal with people, in the way that we handle our finances and in transparency and accountability. We owe it to our people, we owe it to our donors and we owe it to God to be above reproach.

In conclusion, my dream for this great organisation is that The Salvation Army will be characterised as being a force for good, a force for change and a force that lives by the values it proclaims.[16]

Time for reflection

When the last candidate has spoken, the 'getting to know you' process at the High Council has reached its end. Very soon members will have to make a choice, and will each have to decide which of the candidates they consider best fitted to be the next General.

The Council adjourns for a time of further reflection, as determined by the President, and then gathers again for the climax of its deliberations – the election of the next General.

Chapter Nine
Election

EVERYTHING during the days spent at Sunbury Court has led up to this moment. As the Council members take their places at their desks, they know that the time for them to cast their vote for the person of their choice has arrived. The President opens the session with the solemn and time-honoured declaration that has been spoken at all High Councils:

> As we, the members of the High Council, approach the momentous task of electing the next General of The Salvation Army, we do with one accord render glory to the Triune God, Father, Son and Holy Spirit and, in the Name of Jesus Christ our Saviour, invoke the guidance and aid of the Holy Spirit in the discharge of our solemn responsibility, desiring only that the will of God shall be done.[1]

The President then announces that the first ballot will be taken 'for the election and appointment of the _th General of The Salvation Army', and reminds the members of the procedures that will be followed.

As happened in the nomination process, each member in turn and in order of seniority receives from the President or Vice-President an initialled copy of the voting paper that lists the candidates, and walks out to one of the voting rooms. In the privacy of the voting room it is not unusual for members to spend a moment in prayer before placing a tick/check against the name of the person of their choice. Some cast their vote upon their knees. As they in turn come back to the council chamber they place their voting papers in one of the two ballot boxes situated centrally. Apart from the calling out of names and the movement of members there is complete stillness in the council chamber. There is no rush. The process can take up to 45 minutes for each ballot.

When the last member has voted, the four tellers take the ballot boxes into one of the voting rooms and count the votes. The members of the High Council remain seated in silence until the tellers return and hand the result to the President. After a moment the President reads out the voting figures. Members jot them down as they hear them. If one of the candidates has achieved the necessary two-thirds majority, the President announces formally that a General has been elected. If no candidate has reached the required majority, the President announces that the vote has been inconclusive and that after an interval for reflection a further ballot will be taken. Subsequent ballots follow the same procedure.

The first ballot

The announcement of the result of the first ballot is one of the most crucial moments of a High Council for it is the first indication that members have of their corporate thinking as a group. The members may have been together for a week or more, but there have been no opinion polls to predict trends of thinking. Any conversations between them on the subject will have been guarded with very few, if any, sharing with each other how they will vote. The suspense is therefore great and the result can sometimes come as a complete surprise.

In the early High Councils, if the first ballot had been inconclusive, the President read out only the names of the candidates in the order in which the vote had placed them but without disclosing the actual voting figures. The idea appears to have been to give members a preliminary view of the corporate thinking of the Council before more detailed disclosures were made in the second and any subsequent ballots. The 1963 High Council, however, felt that it would be more helpful to have the full voting picture from the start and changed the *Orders of Procedure* accordingly. Since that time the President has announced the individual voting figures for each of the ballots.

The candidates and the other members study the result of the first ballot with great care. Not only does it give the overall picture of the thinking of the High Council, but it also reveals to the individual candidates how many members see them as their *first* choice for the office of General. That can be sobering. It has also happened that a candidate receives no votes at all, which means that even those who originally nominated that person withdrew their support – perhaps in consequence of answers given to questions or the content of the speech made.

The first ballot of course also reveals which candidate has the greatest support. This is an important pointer to the final result. In all but one of the 18 High Councils held to date, the candidate with the most votes in the first ballot has been elected General, either there and then in the first ballot or in a subsequent ballot.

The first ballot furthermore shows the relative strength of all the other participants in the electoral process and it is not unusual for candidates who have received very few votes to voluntarily withdraw from the election at this point.

Before and after 1980

The Salvation Army Act 1980 marks a clear 'before and after' division when it comes to the rules for voting at a High Council.

Before 1980, when the High Council was governed by the 1904 Supplementary Deed, the voting rules required a candidate to obtain a 'two-thirds majority of those voting' in order to be elected General. As many ballots as necessary had to be held until a candidate reached that figure. There was no rule requiring candidates with low votes to withdraw from the process but they were of course at liberty to do so at any time.

The possibility that a High Council might become permanently deadlocked, with no one achieving a two-thirds majority despite repeated ballots, was a constant concern before 1980. Successive High Councils grappled with this issue in their discussions about the *Orders of Procedure*. At various High Councils it was proposed in the discussions on procedures that the candidate receiving the lowest number of votes in each ballot should be *required* to withdraw in order to make deadlock less likely. These proposals were always defeated on the grounds that the 1904 Supplementary Deed did not specify such a procedure. The concern about the possibility of deadlock therefore remained.

There were valid grounds for the concern. Historically it was known that Vatican conclaves in centuries past had sometimes been deadlocked for many months. Though that was unlikely to occur with a High Council, the danger of a High Council some day reaching an impasse could not entirely be ruled out. As it happens, only one pre-1980 High Council reached even five ballots, but this was no guarantee that a deadlock would never occur.

When the Salvation Army Act 1980 was being drafted the opportunity was therefore taken to build in safeguards against possible deadlock. By the new rules, set out in Schedule 4 of that Act, a more than two-thirds majority is required only for the first three ballots. From the fourth ballot onwards, a simple majority of 'more than half of the Council members present' is sufficient for election to take place.

A further change introduced through the 1980 Act to minimise the danger of deadlock is that 'an individual receiving the fewest votes in any ballot of three or more candidates' must withdraw and 'shall not be eligible for any subsequent ballot of that High Council'.

These two changes to the voting rules virtually guarantee that there will be no delay in the electoral process. After the long preparatory build-up towards the election at the High Council, the verdict comes quickly.

The departure from the two-thirds majority requirement was viewed with apprehension by some. General Frederick Coutts had written in 1976: 'The requirement of a two-thirds majority ensures that the elected nominee represents a reasonable consensus of opinion. No one is elected on a marginal vote. No electoral jugglery can transform a minority vote into a decisive majority.'[2] Though retired when the Salvation Army Act 1980 was being drafted, General Coutts voiced his concern to General Arnold Brown about the change being proposed in the new Act. However, there was a consensus view among the Army's leaders in active service at the time that the danger of deadlock outweighed the danger of a General being elected on a marginal vote.

Since 1980 several Generals have in fact been elected without a two-thirds majority and have achieved office on a simple majority vote. The margin by which they have been elected has sometimes been very small. However, any fears that this would inhibit their leadership have proved groundless. The tradition that once a General is elected *everyone* gives the new leader 100 per cent support has proved itself true in practice whether he or she was elected by unanimous vote or by the slenderest of margins.

More than once since 1980 the eventual outcome of the election has become clear by the second or third ballot but without the leading candidate having the necessary two-thirds majority for election. In such cases it has therefore been necessary to continue balloting until the fourth ballot in which a simple majority is sufficient for election.

No deadlock

With the changes introduced in 1980 it is virtually impossible for a High Council to become deadlocked in a way that cannot be resolved. However, a difficult situation could potentially arise even in the fourth ballot and beyond if the two final candidates were to tie or some members were to abstain from the election process by casting blank votes.

Until 1980 it was necessary for a candidate to get a two-thirds majority 'of the members *voting*'. From 1980 onwards, however, a candidate is required to obtain, from the fourth ballot onwards, the votes of more than half 'of the members *present*'. The difference between 'members voting' and 'members present' is hugely significant. It is a deliberate safeguard that has been built into the system through the Salvation Army Act 1980 to counterbalance the dangers entailed in lowering the electoral bar to one of simple majority. No one can be elected General without having the active support of more than half of the Army's leaders.

In a High Council of, say, 100 members, a candidate *must* have the votes of 51 of those members to be elected General. A ballot in which Candidate A receives 50 votes and Candidate B receives 49 votes and one member abstains by casting a blank vote does not result in Candidate A being elected General.

The difficulty is fortunately more theoretical than real. The likelihood of members abstaining in the actual election is remote. The candidates who remain in the fourth and any subsequent ballots will not be the *first* choice of some members, but members know that in the electoral process – as contrasted with the nomination process – they are expected to exercise the right and privilege of casting a vote in each ballot. It is, after all, for that express purpose that they are present at the High Council. And in the 18 High Councils that have been held the total number of blank votes cast has been minimal.

The likelihood of a tie between the two final candidates is also statistically small, but in one post-1980 High Council it did occur on the fourth ballot, which everyone had assumed would be the final ballot. It was therefore necessary to hold a fifth ballot, and the movement of votes in that ballot was sufficient for election to be achieved.

However, provision has to be made in the *Orders of Procedure* for every contingency, including the unlikely possibility of deadlock, and in what has been well described as every President's nightmare paragraph, the following statement is made:

> If, following a fourth ballot, a situation should arise in which no candidate, despite repeated balloting, is able to secure the votes of more than half of the Council members present, the President may provide opportunity for further nominations to be made, including that of an officer who has previously declined nomination or who, having accepted nomination, subsequently and voluntarily withdrew from the

> election. Candidates who had to withdraw from the election because they received the fewest votes in a ballot are not eligible by the terms of Schedule 4 of the Salvation Army Act 1980 to return to the election. Such additional nominations shall be subject to the same procedure as the original nominations.

This provision has never yet been activated, and as it is far from clear how well it would function in practice it is the fervent prayer of every President that it never will be. The provision has the same function as a fire extinguisher that *must* be in place in case of fire – but which hopefully will never need to be used.[3]

Self-votes

In the electoral process the candidates have to decide how they themselves will vote. The rules lay down that no one can nominate himself or herself, but are silent on the question of whether candidates can *vote* for themselves. In a political election it is taken for granted that candidates will do so. For them not to believe in their own candidacy and vote for an opponent instead would be thought very odd.

The question has arisen as to whether the dynamics should be different in a spiritual exercise. General Frederick Coutts could record for our approval in his autobiography that he had never voted for himself, adding that 'no man is fit to judge in his own cause'.[4] Should that be the rule?

The question has taken on a new importance since the introduction of simple majority voting in 1980. With the possibility that a General can be elected by the narrowest of margins, the outcome of an election could theoretically be decided by Candidate A voting for himself or herself and Candidate B out of modesty also voting for Candidate A.

The matter has been discussed at successive High Councils and the informal guidance now given to candidates is as follows: Whether candidates vote for themselves or not is ultimately left to their own discretion, but the general expectation is that they *will* vote for themselves, if only to avoid the danger of the final result being distorted.

A General is elected

In the typical High Council we are observing, the electoral process – whether by one ballot only or by a succession of ballots – now moves to its climax.

The moment comes when the President, after reading out the votes received by the candidates, declares that an election has taken place and announces the name of the General-elect.

This invariably is the trigger for the members of the High Council to burst into warm applause. The Army has its next General! Whether elected by a large or a small majority the members indicate by their sustained clapping that, whatever way they themselves may have voted, their allegiance, their prayers and their hopes are now centred on the General-elect.

Some Generals have shared their thoughts and feelings about that moment. General Albert Orsborn writes:

> It is one of my blessings, given not acquired, that in any kind of crisis I go cool, not hot! This has been helpful many times, but never more so than when the President summoned me to the dais, to be recognised and installed as the General-elect. I can testify that the Spirit of God came upon me, and I heard his 'Amen' in my heart. I was not elated: this was not a victory, since I had not done anything nor had I competed with anyone, to attain this position. It struck me as a conferment, a trust, not an attainment.[5]

General Clarence Wiseman opens his heart and tells of the time when he was declared the General-elect:

> I had difficulty controlling my emotions. For one dramatic moment I needed desperately the inward assurance that I *was* 'the deputy elected by the Lord', that my fellow councillors *had* been led by God, that I *could* depend on his grace and strength for a task I knew to be far

beyond my human competence. In that fleeting fraction of time the Lord brought to my mind like a shaft of light an inspired phrase from a cherished hymn: 'I cast my load on timeless grace'.[6]

About my own experience I write in my autobiography: 'When it came to the time for voting, Freda and I had a profound sense of peace in our hearts. Our times were in God's hands, and from our personal perspective, whatever the outcome it would be fine with us. We entered into the first ballot. When the President announced the result I found that I had achieved the necessary two-thirds majority in the first ballot – and had therefore been elected the next General of The Salvation Army. There comes a moment when theorising about "what might be" suddenly changes into hard fact. I can remember the awesome realisation hitting me in that moment that I was about to step into the shoes of William Booth himself.'[7]

The will of God

All High Councils have rightly prayed that in their exercise of spiritual discernment the will of God may be done. However, in that beautiful and evocative phrase lies a dilemma with which many High Council members have wrestled. Unless the High Council is unanimous in its election – which has happened only once – does it mean that those who did not vote for the new General were unable to perceive the will of God? Also, what if the High Council finds itself deeply divided in the final vote as has now happened on several occasions? Does it mean that nearly half of the High Council was unable to grasp what God wanted?

There are no easy answers to that dilemma. Any writing about the will of God is fraught with difficulties for by definition it is a subject beyond human knowledge. However, the previously mentioned words of St Augustine – 'without God we cannot; without us God will not' – help us to understand that in the choices that have to be made we humans play a large and inescapable role. The exercise of spiritual discernment is not to seek to discern the person whom God has already chosen, but is a spiritual and intellectual exercise to seek to discern who among the candidates is the right leader for the Army for that particular time. In every High Council more than one candidate has had the qualities to make a good General, and in the exercise of discernment it is entirely legitimate that there should be differences of opinion.

To return to an analogy already mentioned, the High Council is like a territorial appointments board that is seeking to find the most qualified officer to lead the largest corps in the territory. In its discussions, it becomes clear to the board that a number of officers have the necessary qualities and that each would bring some special – and perhaps even unique – giftedness to the appointment. Views may differ as to which of these unique qualities or gift mixes is the most relevant. But the board does not think in terms of seeking to discover the officer that God has already chosen. The board members know that the responsibility for making a judgement rests with them. However, when after much prayer and thought the choice is finally made, the board unites in support of the decision and prays – and trusts – that the choice it has made will be an expression of the will of God for that corps and for that officer.

Parallel dynamics operate in a High Council. Everyone knows that Candidates A, B and C can bring valuable qualities to bear on the office of General. It is entirely legitimate that differences of opinion should exist as to which qualities are the most important. The thinking and discussion and voting are bathed in prayer. When a final decision is reached through the election process the High Council as a whole accepts the result of the voting. The Council unites behind the choice it has made and, even when there have been divergences of views, dares to believe that God will bless its choice of a new General and dares to affirm that in *that* sense the selection it has made is an expression of the will of God.

No one has better expressed this dilemma and pointed to its solution than General Albert Orsborn. He writes of his experience at the 1946 High Council as the balloting proceeded: 'I truly felt the spiritual submission and obedience of the whole council to know and to do the will of God. I was never able to accept as a fact that the will of the majority, even of good men, was necessarily the will of God. I certainly *hoped* it would be so. I expected that our honest mistakes would be eliminated as the voting proceeded. I was from the beginning prepared to accept the final result, no matter what, as the will of God. All of us would then need to work together in that belief.'[8]

All High Councils have indeed gone out and worked together in that belief. Whatever divergences there may have been on the way, or even in the final ballot, successive High Councils have been able to echo with one voice the testimony of the Council of Jerusalem, which at the end of its deliberations announced its findings with the words: 'It seemed good to the Holy Spirit and to us...' (Acts 15:28 *New International Version*).

At the High Council we are observing, Council members have done what seemed good to the Holy Spirit and to them. They have made a choice – but their choice has yet to be revealed to the world.

Chapter Ten

Revelation

THE first sign that a new pope has been elected is when white smoke issues from a small chimney that is visible to the crowd gathered in St Peter's Square in Rome. A chemical has been added to the small stove just off the Sistine Chapel in which the ballot papers are burned and this ensures that the message cannot be mistaken. The crowd greets the white smoke with joyful cries: 'We have a pope!'

To any observers in the grounds of Sunbury Court, the first indication that a new General has been elected is much more prosaic. The electrically operated blinds shielding the large floor-to-ceiling windows of the council chamber begin a majestic descent until the inside of the chamber is hidden from view. The recorder knows that to press the button is one of his tasks as soon as the President announces that a General has been elected. The descent of the blinds ensures that what happens next will not be observed by any passers-by.

Following the applause that greeted the announcement of the name of the next General, the President calls the officer elected to the dais, if married together with his/her spouse, and, as required by Schedule 4 of the Salvation Army Act 1980, asks that person formally whether he or she will accept office. An affirmative response from the person elected will indicate his or her willingness to sign the Deed of Acceptance of the Office of General.

Curiously, Schedule 4 permits the person elected to delay acceptance of office for 24 hours should he or she so wish. This has never yet happened, but should it ever happen, the High Council would have to remain in being during the 24-hour period. If following that period the person elected had still not yet accepted office, 'his election shall be void' and the High Council would have to start from the beginning again.

As I comment in my autobiography: 'It is difficult to imagine what could motivate someone elected as General to ask for a delay at this point, but it is not hard to picture the cataclysmic effect that a delay would have on the members of the High Council and on the Army around the world. Fortunately no one elected as General has ever wished to take advantage of this route for delay – or escape.'[1]

The 24-hour provision for delay appears to have been included in Schedule 4 more to meet some unforeseeable or even unimaginable contingency – say, that the person elected has been hindered from being physically present at the High Council – than to give time for anyone who has just been through a long electoral process to make up his or her mind whether or not to accept election.

When the officer elected to be the next General responds to the President that he or she is willing to accept office, the President declares that officer to be 'duly elected' and formally announces:

> In the ballot taken this…day of…(month, year) for the election of the General of The Salvation Army,…has been duly elected in accordance with the requirements of the Salvation Army Act 1980 as the _th General of The Salvation Army.

The formal announcement leads to another ovation, which also helps to further dispel any tension there may have been in the election process and which readies the ground for a series of happenings both formal and informal. Among these happenings will always be prayers of dedication and thanksgiving – sometimes with congregational singing – together with prayers for the General-elect. The order in which the various items are taken in these final moments of the High Council is at the discretion of the President and has varied between High Councils.

The recorder by mobile phone asks the legal adviser to come to the council chamber. The President is required by the Act to notify the General-in-office of the name of the General-elect, and takes the opportunity to do so in a private phone conversation from within the chamber as early as possible in the post-election proceedings.

Signing of the Deed of Acceptance

When all is set the President calls on the members of the High Council to stand for the signing of the Deed of Acceptance of the Office of General of The Salvation Army. With the legal adviser in attendance the President asks the General-elect to read out the solemn words of the deed – as set out in Schedule 7 of the Salvation Army Act 1980:

DEED OF ACCEPTANCE OF THE OFFICE OF GENERAL

TO ALL TO WHOM THESE PRESENTS SHALL COME I [name of the person elected], General-elect of The Salvation Army SEND GREETING:

WHEREAS by paragraph 15 of Schedule 4 to the Salvation Army Act 1980 ('the Act') it is provided that every person elected as General of The Salvation Army shall, immediately upon notification to him of such election, execute a deed in the form set out in Schedule 7 to the Act

AND WHEREAS on the...day of...at a meeting of the High Council of The Salvation Army held at...I was duly elected to be General of The Salvation Army in succession to [name of predecessor] upon his [retiring] on the...day of... or upon the sooner happening of any event by which his office should otherwise be vacated and the fact of my election has been duly communicated to me in accordance with the provisions of the Act

NOW THESE PRESENTS WITNESS as follows:

1. In pursuance of paragraph 15 of Schedule 4 to the Act and for the purpose of complying therewith I DO BY THIS DEED under my hand and seal ACCEPT the office of General of The Salvation Army in

succession to the said [name of predecessor] upon and subject to the provisions of the Salvation Army Acts 1931 to 1980.

2. I hereby undertake not to resign from the office of General of The Salvation Army during the period of twenty-four months from the date hereof save in circumstances in which I consider my resignation unavoidable, whether for reasons of illness or otherwise.

3. I hereby declare that any property, right or interest which becomes vested in me as General of The Salvation Army shall, unless vested subject to any other trust, be held by me in trust for The Salvation Army.

IN WITNESS whereof I the said [name of General-elect] have hereunto set my hand and seal this...day of...

SIGNED, SEALED AND DELIVERED by the said [name of General-elect] in the presence of: (the legal adviser).

After the General-elect has read the words of the Deed of Acceptance, the President invites him/her to sign the deed. The legal adviser signs as a witness. A copy of this certificate is later sent to those territories and commands that require it for legal purposes.

The President, Vice-President and two senior commissioners then sign a Certificate of the Proceedings of the High Council, witnessed by two other commissioners, certifying that the General-elect has been duly elected.

With the signing of the Deed of Acceptance all legalities required by the Salvation Army Act 1980 have been observed. The person elected is now truly and properly the General-elect. The High Council has fulfilled its function and as the Act succinctly puts it: 'Immediately after the President has notified the person elected of his election as General and such person has so accepted office, the proceedings of the High Council shall terminate and it shall thereupon stand dissolved.'

In its legal aspects the High Council may have come to an end – but much has still to happen. And as the High Council enters a more informal stage, to the fore come the notes of spontaneity, warmth and joy that mark Salvation Army welcomes everywhere.

The General-elect speaks

The members of the High Council look forward to hearing their new leader, and usually following the signing of the official documents the President invites the General-elect to speak.

General Albert Orsborn writes of this moment in the 1946 High Council: 'I had no prepared speech. I just made a simple statement about my trust, likening it to the water brought by valiant men from the well by Bethlehem gate to David. He would not drink of it, because it cost the lives of men, but poured it out as an oblation before the Lord. So, I thought, the honour of our generalship had been given to others, and to me, because of the devotion and sacrifice of God's people. It was not a personal honour; I would not receive it as such. It must be accepted in humility and poured out upon the altar.'[2]

General Wilfred Kitching recalls his inward reaction at that point in the 1954 High Council: 'Having realised by the way that the voting was going it seemed as though I would be elected as the General and that some words of acceptance would be expected of me, I had hurriedly written a few notes on a sheet of paper. As I handle that small scrap of paper and reread the hurried notes, all the emotion and fears of that sacred moment are easily recalled. To leave my seat in the Council chamber at the behest of the President and to stand before those who had given me their support, as well as 14 others who had been led to vote for another, was to know that from that moment far greater demands would be made on me than ever before. Only God's grace would suffice.'[3]

General Arnold Brown in 1977 said: 'I follow in a distinguished succession. I can never hope to be a William Booth or a Bramwell Booth, or indeed any of their successors. But I remember that after the assassination of Dr Martin Luther King, somebody said to Dr Ralph Abernathy: "Will you be able to fill Dr Martin Luther King's shoes?" To that he replied: "I am afraid not, but I have a pair of my own." I am not sure that I will be able to fill the shoes of any of the great leaders who have gone before, but I have some sandals of my own.'[4]

General George Carpenter's words of acceptance in 1939 have become classic. He concluded with:

> My comrades, I do not expect that by reason of my acceptance of this high responsibility – this place of privilege also – I do not expect by that fact to be changed into another man. In and by the grace of God, I am what all the days that have gone before have made me.
>
> I promise you that I will walk humbly with my God; that I will seek to be an example in all the qualities that you regard as precious in the life of the Army – an example in simplicity, in faith, in sacrifice, an example in courage and in direct personal witness for Christ.[5]

A personal moment with the General-elect

Traditionally all members have a personal moment with the General-elect and this is usually linked with them each signing in order of seniority the Certificate of Election and Appointment that is to be presented to the new international leader.

While the General-elect, and spouse if he/she is married, stand near the front the President invites members to come forward to greet them before they sign the Certificate. The effect of this invitation has often been the same as when the leader of any Salvation Army meeting calls on members of the congregation to stand up and go and greet someone in the hall. Members rise from their seats and move around greeting each other with hugs and handshakes. For the next 30 minutes or so there are unrestrained and delightful moments of joyful fellowship as members celebrate with each other the accomplishing of their mission.

A queue of members waiting to greet the General-elect soon builds up, but members also make sure they have a personal word with the other candidates who have taken part in the election to thank them for standing and to wish them well.

General Eva Burrows tells of the moment at the 1986 High Council: 'One of the beautiful things at the High Council is that once the General is elected, total loyalty is expressed. When the final vote was counted, I was called to come to the head of the table and, following a prayer, each of the members came to greet me, sharing a personal word of encouragement and support. And those who had themselves been nominated said in a very deliberate way, "I give you my total loyalty". It was a very moving experience. There had been no lobbying, no competition; it was all conducted in the spirit of love and unity.'[6]

General Shaw Clifton has described to an interviewer his own experience at the 2006 High Council, at which he was elected, of 'the very beautiful gathering around the one who becomes the General-elect' that occurs at this point. 'At the end of the proceedings there is a beautiful process for everybody affirming that person. I found that such a humbling, loving experience to go through. However you have cast your vote there is an opportunity to affirm the new General-elect. The whole company does that – they do it one by one – and that's done by an embrace, a handshake, a personal word of affirmation, and time is given for all of that to happen.'[7]

Certificate of Election and Appointment

The tradition of presenting a Certificate of Election and Appointment signed by all members of the Council, dates back to the 1954 High Council and is a tangible way by which all members can express their solidarity with their newly elected leader. Each member in due course receives a photocopy. The certificate traditionally reads:

> ELECTION AND APPOINTMENT OF THE GENERAL
>
> Whereas the … High Council of The Salvation Army meeting at Sunbury Court has today elected [name of General-elect] as General of The Salvation Army, in succession to [name of predecessor], those whose names here follow sign this Certificate of Election as an assurance of their united love and loyalty, praying that God's continued presence and guidance may be vouchsafed to the Army for the salvation of souls and the extension of his Kingdom. God bless the General!

As the High Council draws to its conclusion, the President leads a further song of dedication after which the final prayer is offered.

It is now time to meet the world.

Opening the door

Word that a General has been elected has been passed out from the council chamber and a group of officers and Salvationists together with the High Council support staff have gathered outside the closed door of the meeting room. With the blinds being closed those outside cannot see what is happening within the council chamber.

As described in the opening paragraphs of this book, it is not only the group standing outside that is present at this moment. Through the marvels of modern technology, thousands of Salvationists all around the world are also watching the closed door as the event is webcast on the Internet. Soon the identity of the next General of The Salvation Army will be revealed.

Heading the welcome group is the General-in-office. The happy tradition whereby the first non-member to greet the next General is the General-in-office has only become a fixed point in more recent High Councils.

With the 2006 High Council being a winter High Council – the first since 1929 – it became necessary to change what had become the pattern since the opening of the new conference suite. When the doors opened, instead of the President leading the General-elect out to the microphone placed on the grass followed by the members of the High Council, the President invited everyone – including the cameras – into the council chamber where he presented the General-elect to the General-in-office and to the watching world. This pattern was followed again in 2011. In 2013 the President led the new General to a microphone placed in the foyer outside the meeting room before presenting him to those gathered and to the worldwide Salvationist family.

Whether outside or inside the council chamber, the General-in-office also expresses words of welcome, garlands and flowers are presented and the General-elect for the first time speaks words of greeting to Salvationists around the globe. The short ceremony closes with prayer.

The final voting figures are not disclosed at the time of the announcement. For the first five High Councils the figures were made known in the bulletin announcing the name of the General-elect, and these are included in *The History of The Salvation Army*.[8] The 1963 High Council set the pattern whereby only the number of ballots was made public but not the actual voting figures. There are strong grounds for this policy – even more so since 1980 when Generals can be elected on a simple majority vote – for what counts is that The Salvation Army has a new General, not whether he or she became General by a large or small majority. It would also be impossible to convey to distant observers around the world the total and absolute rallying around the new General that occurs at a High Council however great or slender his or her majority in the final ballot.

However, there is a legitimate historical interest in such matters, and with voting figures before 1963 having been quoted in subsequent official histories, the 2002 High Council felt that the balance of interests would best be served if a time limit were set for the release of this information to future historians. The *Orders of Procedure* therefore now decree that 'the voting figures and number of ballots shall not be disclosed within a period of 10 years, except for essential legal purposes'.

The news of the General's election goes far beyond the Salvationist family. The media are informed and the General-elect is soon caught up with telephone interviews and requests for on-camera exchanges. 'Within minutes of signing the Deed of Acceptance,' recalls General Arnold Brown, 'I was in front of television and film cameras which were probing not only the shape of a General-elect's face but, hopefully, the shape of his mind. I had the discomfiting sensation of having been catapulted from a joyous equality shared around the green, baize-covered tables by all councillors into an almost frightening "alone-ness", somewhere beyond the state of *primus inter pares*.'[9]

A great advance made in the history of the High Council is that nowadays the spouse of a married General-elect is there to share the moment. Until 1999 that was not so. In his account of the final moments of the 1977 High Council, General Arnold Brown describes how his inner turmoil at being elected 'was increased by anxiety as to how "the news" could be conveyed to my wife, at that moment 37,000 feet in the air flying back from women's rallies held further away from Toronto – yet still in our command – than Toronto is from London'.[10] In retrospect it is now difficult to comprehend that it took 70 years of High Council history for that dilemma – faced by all married Generals-elect – to be resolved.

A recurring surprise for High Council members is how quickly the Council breaks up after the announcement of the new General. They have been together for many days and the pace has often been tranquil and reflective. Yet the end comes with a sudden abruptness. The President usually declares the next meal to be the official farewell meal. The General-in-office and the General-elect preside at this meal. Brief words of thanks and farewell are spoken. Then it is time for members to say goodbye to each other and head for the airports. The High Council is over.

The new reality

The members of the High Council depart but a thousand and one things await the attention of the General-elect. He or she faces a new and inescapable reality. The media will not be slow to explore every angle of that reality – not always getting it right.

General Wilfred Kitching relates that after his election in 1954 a newspaper behind the Iron Curtain, in a land where the Army flag had once flown, gave a graphic description of his election and informed its readers that the new General 'led an army of five million soldiers, all of whom were pledged to sleep with the bedroom window open, eat their vegetables uncooked, and as far as possible have a cold bath every morning'.[11]

Even internal communications can break down. General Arnold Brown tells of how 'there was a moment of relieving humour when it was learned that the Chief of the Staff's cabled notification to territories and commands around the world had suffered a distortion in transmission. The message as released read: "Brown elected. God bless the General." Alas, a full stop was misplaced, so that one leading officer read with understandable incredulity: "Brown elected God. Bless the General".'[12]

The interval of around seven weeks between the High Council and taking office races by for the General-elect as he or she prepares to leave one appointment and take up the next. All too soon the moment for entering into the responsibilities of office arrives. Let that prince among Salvationist autobiographers, General Albert Orsborn, have the last word as he describes his thoughts and feelings on that first day of his generalship – 21 June 1946:

> This is the date that is indelibly imprinted on my soul! Never shall I forget the sense of awe and indescribable responsibility that came upon me as I entered the office at Denmark Hill [where International Headquarters was located following the destruction of its premises in 101 Queen Victoria Street during the Second World War]. I remember trembling, and feeling lonely. I was not actually alone, for no man was ever surrounded and upheld by more willing and loyal comrades. I knew I had wonderful support; nevertheless, it suddenly came home to me, with weighty impact, that the supreme, the ultimate leadership of a worldwide Army of God was now upon me! There was no escape, no way of compromise, I must take up the task and go forward. Hitherto in my career I had been able to appeal for guidance to the leader above me. Now, there was no one above me; I had been raised to the position of a final Court of Appeal. I could take advice, but decisions must be mine. It was a solemnising, even a frightening thought.'[13]

Like every General before him and after him, General Albert Orsborn will have thanked God for the knowledge that hundreds of thousands of Salvationists around the world were upholding him in prayer. In the strength of those prayers, the General of The Salvation Army – whoever he or she may be – can face the realities of today and tomorrow with confidence.

Appendix

High Council Data 1929-2013

Notes

- The venue for all but three of the High Councils has been Sunbury Court. The High Councils of 1934 and 1939 were held at the Clapton Centre. The 2013 High Council was held at the Renaissance Hotel, near Heathrow, because Sunbury Court was being refurbished at the time.
- The dates and length of High Councils include Sundays and any other adjournments.
- The 1929 High Council dealt with a constitutional crisis and was therefore significantly longer.
- The acronym 'CoS' stands for Chief of the Staff.

1929 HIGH COUNCIL
General Edward Higgins elected

Date: Tuesday 8 January to Wednesday 13 February 1929 – with adjournments
Length: 37 days
Number of members: 63
President: Commissioner James Hay
Vice-President: Lieut-Commissioner William Haines

Nominees:
Commissioner Catherine Booth
Commander Evangeline Booth
Commissioner James Hay
Commissioner Edward Higgins (CoS)
Commissioner Samuel Hurren
Commissioner Henry Mapp
Lieut-Commissioner Charles Rich

Candidates:
Commander Evangeline Booth
Commissioner Edward Higgins

1934 HIGH COUNCIL
General Evangeline Booth elected

Date: Tuesday 28 August to Monday 3 September 1934
Length: 7 days
Number of members: 47
President: Commissioner Karl Larsson
Vice-President: Lieut-Commissioner George Carpenter

Nominees:
Commander Evangeline Booth
Commissioner Catherine Bramwell-Booth
Commissioner James Hay
Commissioner Samuel Hurren
Commissioner David Lamb
Commissioner Henry Mapp (CoS)
Commissioner John McMillan

Candidates:
Commander Evangeline Booth
Commissioner Catherine Bramwell-Booth
Commissioner Samuel Hurren
Commissioner David Lamb
Commissioner Henry Mapp

1939 HIGH COUNCIL
General George Carpenter elected

Date: Tuesday 15 August to Thursday 24 August 1939
Length: 10 days
Number of members: 51
President: Commissioner Edward Parker
Vice-President: Commissioner Charles Baugh

Nominees:
Commissioner Charles Baugh
Commissioner Catherine Bramwell-Booth
Commissioner George Carpenter
Commissioner Alfred Cunningham
Lieut-Commissioner William Dalziel
Commissioner Alexander Damon
Commissioner Samuel Hurren
Commissioner John McMillan (CoS)
Commissioner Benjamin Orames
Lieut-Commissioner Albert Orsborn

Candidates:
Commissioner Catherine Bramwell-Booth
Commissioner George Carpenter
Lieut-Commissioner William Dalziel
Commissioner Benjamin Orames
Lieut-Commissioner Albert Orsborn

1946 HIGH COUNCIL
General Albert Orsborn elected

Date: Thursday 25 April to Thursday 9 May 1946
Length: 15 days
Number of members: 47
President: Commissioner Frank Dyer
Vice-President: Lieut-Commissioner Norman Marshall followed by Lieut-Commissioner Ejner Thykjaer

Nominees:
Commissioner Frank Barrett
Commissioner Charles Baugh (CoS)
Commissioner Catherine Bramwell-Booth
Commissioner William Dalziel
Lieut-Commissioner Norman Marshall
Commissioner William Maxwell
Commissioner Donald McMillan
Lieut-Commissioner Tobias Ögrim
Commissioner Benjamin Orames
Commissioner Albert Orsborn
Commissioner Ernest Pugmire
Commissioner Phillis Taylor

Candidates:
Commissioner Frank Barrett
Commissioner Charles Baugh
Commissioner Catherine Bramwell-Booth
Commissioner William Dalziel
Lieut-Commissioner Norman Marshall
Commissioner William Maxwell
Commissioner Benjamin Orames
Commissioner Albert Orsborn

1954 HIGH COUNCIL
General Wilfred Kitching elected

Date: Thursday 29 April to Tuesday 11 May 1954
Length: 13 days
Number of members: 46
President: Commissioner William Dalziel
Vice-Presidents: Commissioner Emma Davies and Commissioner Ejner Thykjaer

Nominees:
Commissioner John J. Allan
Lieut-Commissioner Wycliffe Booth
Commissioner Edgar Dibden (CoS)
Commissioner Wilfred Kitching
Commissioner Herbert Lord
Commissioner Norman Marshall
General Albert Orsborn

Candidates:
Lieut-Commissioner Wycliffe Booth
Commissioner Wilfred Kitching
Commissioner Herbert Lord
Commissioner Norman Marshall

1963 HIGH COUNCIL
General Frederick Coutts elected

Date: Thursday 19 September to Tuesday 1 October 1963
Length: 13 days
Number of members: 49
President: Commissioner Norman Marshall
Vice-President: Commissioner Owen Culshaw

Nominees:
Commissioner Wycliffe Booth
Commissioner Frederick Coutts
Commissioner Edgar Grinsted
Commissioner Glenn R. Ryan
Commissioner Erik Wickberg (CoS)
Lieut-Commissioner Clarence Wiseman

Candidates:
Commissioner Wycliffe Booth
Commissioner Frederick Coutts
Commissioner Edgar Grinsted
Commissioner Glenn R. Ryan
Commissioner Erik Wickberg
Lieut-Commissioner Clarence Wiseman

1969 HIGH COUNCIL
General Erik Wickberg elected

Date: Thursday 17 July to Wednesday 23 July 1969
Length: 7 days
Number of members: 45
President: Commissioner Hubert Scotney
Vice-President: Commissioner Samuel Hepburn

Nominees:
Commissioner Edward Carey
Commissioner Francis Evans
Commissioner Albert Mingay
Commissioner Hubert Scotney
Commissioner Kaare Westergaard
Commissioner Erik Wickberg (CoS)
Commissioner Clarence Wiseman

Candidates:
Commissioner Kaare Westergaard
Commissioner Erik Wickberg

1974 HIGH COUNCIL
General Clarence Wiseman elected

Date: Saturday 4 May to Monday 13 May 1974
Length: 10 days
Number of members: 40
President: Commissioner Clarence Wiseman followed by Commissioner Francis Evans
Vice-President: Commissioner Francis Evans followed by Commissioner Paul Carlson

Nominees:
Commissioner Arnold Brown (CoS)
Commissioner Geoffrey Dalziel
Commissioner Paul S. Kaiser
Commissioner Leslie Pindred
Commissioner Bramwell Tripp
Commissioner Clarence Wiseman

Candidates:
Commissioner Arnold Brown
Commissioner Geoffrey Dalziel
Commissioner Paul S. Kaiser
Commissioner Clarence Wiseman

1977 HIGH COUNCIL
General Arnold Brown elected

Date: Friday 29 April to Thursday 5 May 1977
Length: 7 days
Number of members: 41
President: Commissioner J. Bramwell Tripp
Vice-President: Commissioner Leslie Pindred

Nominees:
Commissioner Arnold Brown
Commissioner Stanley Cottrill
Commissioner Geoffrey Dalziel
Commissioner Harry Williams

Candidates:
Commissioner Arnold Brown
Commissioner Harry Williams

1981 HIGH COUNCIL
General Jarl Wahlström elected

Date: Friday 16 October to Friday 23 October 1981
Length: 8 days
Number of members: 44
President: Commissioner William Goodier
Vice-President: Commissioner Eva Burrows

Nominees:
Commissioner Caughey Gauntlett
Commissioner Arthur Holland
Commissioner Denis Hunter
Commissioner Norman S. Marshall
Commissioner John D. Needham
Commissioner George L. Nelting
Commissioner Howard Orsborn
Commissioner Arthur Pitcher
Commissioner Jarl Wahlström

Candidates:
Commissioner Caughey Gauntlett
Commissioner Denis Hunter
Commissioner Norman S. Marshall
Commissioner Howard Orsborn
Commissioner Arthur Pitcher
Commissioner Jarl Wahlström

1986 HIGH COUNCIL
General Eva Burrows elected

Date: Friday 25 April to Friday 2 May 1986
Length: 8 days
Number of members: 46
President: Commissioner Norman S. Marshall
Vice-President: Commissioner Anna Hannevik

Nominees:
Commissioner Eva Burrows
Commissioner Francy Cachelin
Commissioner William Cairns
Commissioner Ron Cox
Commissioner Stanley E. Ditmer
Commissioner Caughey Gauntlett (CoS)
Colonel Wesley Harris
Commissioner Norman S. Marshall
Commissioner Andrew S. Miller
Commissioner William Pratt
Commissioner Harry Read
Commissioner Robert S. Rightmire
Commissioner Mannam Samuel

Candidates:
Commissioner Eva Burrows
Commissioner Francy Cachelin
Commissioner William Cairns
Colonel Wesley Harris
Commissioner Andrew S. Miller
Commissioner Harry Read
Commissioner Mannam Samuel

1993 HIGH COUNCIL
General Bramwell Tillsley elected

Date: Thursday 22 April to Wednesday 28 April 1993
Length: 7 days
Number of members: 50
President: Commissioner James Osborne
Vice-President: Commissioner Wesley Harris

Nominees:
Commissioner Peter Chang
Commissioner John Gowans
Commissioner Kenneth L. Hodder
Commissioner Earle Maxwell
Commissioner James Osborne
Commissioner Dinsdale Pender
Commissioner Paul A. Rader
Commissioner Bramwell Tillsley (CoS)

Candidates:
Commissioner John Gowans
Commissioner Kenneth L. Hodder
Commissioner Earle Maxwell
Commissioner Dinsdale Pender
Commissioner Paul A. Rader
Commissioner Bramwell Tillsley

1994 HIGH COUNCIL
General Paul A. Rader elected

Date: Tuesday 19 July to Saturday 23 July 1994
Length: 5 days
Number of members: 44
President: Commissioner Kenneth L. Hodder
Vice-President: Commissioner John Clinch

Nominees:
Commissioner John Gowans
Commissioner Kenneth L. Hodder
Commissioner Ronald G. Irwin
Commissioner Ah Ang Lim
Commissioner Earle Maxwell (CoS)
Commissioner Paul A. Rader

Candidates:
Commissioner John Gowans
Commissioner Earle Maxwell
Commissioner Paul A. Rader

1999 HIGH COUNCIL
General John Gowans elected

Date: Thursday 6 May to Saturday 15 May 1999
Length: 10 days
Number of members: 74
President: Commissioner Robert A. Watson
Vice-President: Commissioner Verna Skinner

Nominees:
Colonel Shaw Clifton
Commissioner Douglas Davis
Commissioner David Edwards
Colonel Israel L. Gaither
Commissioner John Gowans
Commissioner John Larsson
Commissioner Earle Maxwell (CoS)
Commissioner Robert A. Watson

Candidates:
Colonel Shaw Clifton
Colonel Israel L. Gaither
Commissioner John Gowans
Commissioner John Larsson
Commissioner Earle Maxwell

2002 HIGH COUNCIL
General John Larsson elected

Date: Friday 30 August to Friday 6 September 2002
Length: 8 days
Number of members: 87
President: Commissioner Brian Taylor
Vice-President: Commissioner Linda Bond

Nominees:
Commissioner Shaw Clifton
Commissioner Paul du Plessis
Commissioner Israel L. Gaither
Commissioner Alex Hughes
Commissioner Hasse Kjellgren
Commissioner John Larsson (CoS)
Commissioner Mohan Masih
Commissioner Philip D. Needham
Commissioner Donald Ødegaard

Candidates:
Commissioner Shaw Clifton
Commissioner Hasse Kjellgren
Commissioner John Larsson

2006 HIGH COUNCIL
General Shaw Clifton elected

Date: Friday 20 January to Saturday 28 January 2006
Length: 9 days
Number of members: 100
President: Commissioner W. Todd Bassett
Vice-President: Commissioner Robin Dunster

Nominees:
Commissioner Linda Bond
Commissioner Shaw Clifton
Commissioner Israel L. Gaither (CoS)
Commissioner Hasse Kjellgren
Commissioner Carl Lydholm
Commissioner M. Christine MacMillan
Commissioner Philip D. Needham

Candidates:
Commissioner Shaw Clifton
Commissioner Israel L. Gaither
Commissioner Hasse Kjellgren
Commissioner Carl Lydholm
Commissioner M. Christine MacMillan

2011 HIGH COUNCIL
General Linda Bond elected

Date: Friday 21 January to Monday 31 January 2011
Length: 11 days
Number of members: 109
President: Commissioner William W. Francis followed by Commissioner James M. Knaggs
Vice-President: Commissioner Betty Matear followed by Colonel Birgitte Brekke

Nominees:
Commissioner Linda Bond
Commissioner Maxwell Feener
Commissioner William W. Francis
Commissioner James M. Knaggs
Commissioner Dick Krommenhoek
Commissioner M. Christine MacMillan
Commissioner John Matear
Commissioner William A. Roberts
Commissioner Robert Street
Commissioner Barry C. Swanson (CoS)

Candidates:
Commissioner Linda Bond
Commissioner Maxwell Feener
Commissioner William W. Francis
Commissioner Dick Krommenhoek
Commissioner M. Christine MacMillan
Commissioner John Matear
Commissioner William A. Roberts
Commissioner Robert Street
Commissioner Barry C. Swanson

2013 HIGH COUNCIL
General André Cox elected

Date: Monday 29 July to Saturday 3 August 2013
Length: 6 days
Number of members: 117
President: Commissioner William A. Roberts
Vice-President: Commissioner Birgitte Brekke

Nominees:
Commissioner Clive Adams
Commissioner André Cox (CoS)
Commissioner Kenneth G. Hodder
Commissioner James M. Knaggs
Commissioner Dick Krommenhoek
Commissioner Barry C. Swanson

Candidates:
Commissioner André Cox
Commissioner Kenneth G. Hodder
Commissioner James M. Knaggs
Commissioner Dick Krommenhoek
Commissioner Barry C. Swanson

Notes

Publishers of books are listed in the endnotes only at the first appearance of each book.

Chapter One – Genesis

1 Frederick Coutts, autobiography, *No Continuing City* (Hodder and Stoughton, 1976), page 95.

2 Letter dated 24 November 1927. International Heritage Centre.

3 International Heritage Centre.

4 International Headquarters (IHQ), 2009.

5 William Booth, *A Talk with Mr Gladstone at his own Fireside* (IHQ, 1897), page 33.

6 International Heritage Centre.

7 Frederick Coutts, *The Better Fight: The History of The Salvation Army*, Volume VI 1914-1946 (Hodder and Stoughton, 1973), page 101.

Chapter Two – Members

1 The Chief of the Staff is the most senior of the commissioners by virtue of his position. Seniority for the other commissioners is by the date of promotion to that rank. Seniority for territorial commanders who are colonels is by the date of their appointment as territorial commanders. Married couples sit together.

2 Preliminary Report of the Advisory Commission on Constitutional Reform.

3 Arnold Brown, *The Gate and The Light* (Bookwright Publications, 1984), page 155.

4 The linked Minute by the Chief of the Staff, also of February 2010, which establishes 'that the designation territorial president of women's ministries will be applied solely to the spouse of a territorial commander', also adds that 'where the territorial commander is not married, or has a spouse who is not in active service, the designation territorial president of women's ministries will be either (a) given to the territorial commander; or (b) not used in that instance.'

5 Until 2011 the Chief of the Staff also handled the election of the Vice-President and Chaplain, with the President taking over after the break.

Chapter Three – Procedures

[1] Minutes of the 1939 High Council.

[2] The Commission was chaired by Commissioner Arthur Thompson.

[3] John Gowans, *There's a Boy Here* (IHQ, 2002), page 124.

[4] Karl Larsson, *Under Order* (*Under Orders*), Volume III, (Territorial Headquarters, Sweden, 1951), page 163.

[5] Albert Orsborn, *The House of my Pilgrimage* (Salvationist Publishing and Supplies Ltd (SP&S), 1958), page 144.

[6] In this exchange with Mr Frost and in later quoted material the word 'questions' is used in the sense of 'issues'. In order to draw a clear distinction between 'discussion of issues' and 'questions addressed to candidates', I have taken the liberty of replacing the word 'questions' with 'issues' wherever appropriate in these quotations for the sake of clarity. It should be noted that Mr Frost also sometimes uses the word 'appointment' in the sense of 'appointment by election'.

[7] *Constitutional Notes* prepared for the 1939 High Council by Mr William Frost.

[8] Albert Orsborn, *The House of my Pilgrimage*, page 144.

[9] Clarence D. Wiseman, *A Burning in my Bones* (McGraw-Hill Ryerson Limited, 1979), page 180.

[10] *High Council 2006*. DVD issued by IHQ.

[11] Karl Larsson, *Under Order* (*Under Orders*), Volume III, page 161.

[12] Should the conclave reach an impasse, the constitution provides ways for its resolution. If after seven ballots no one has been elected, the voting is to be suspended for a day of prayer and discussion. This procedure is to be repeated if after seven further ballots the voting is still inconclusive – and repeated again and yet again if necessary. If after 33 ballots no one has secured a two-thirds majority, the cardinals are empowered to narrow the choice to the two top candidates.

Chapter Four – Nominations

[1] Frederick Coutts, *No Continuing City*, page 97.

[2] Ibid, page 97.

Chapter Five – Nominators

[1] Arnold Brown, *The Gate and the Light*, page 157.

[2] Stella O. Carpenter, *A Man of Peace in a World at War* (Private publication, Australia, 1993), page 209.

[3] George Carpenter was a pacifist at heart, and though this would have been known

only to a few members of the 1939 High Council, it remains a further endorsement of the Council's wisdom in electing him to be the international leader at such a sensitive time. See Shaw Clifton, *The Salvation Army's Actions and Attitudes in Wartime: 1899-1945*, Doctor of Philosophy dissertation, University of London 1988, pages 345-347.

4 The age of retirement of the General is determined by *Orders and Regulations Governing the Age of Retirement of the General and an Extension of the General's Term of Office*. These regulations may be varied by the General with the consent of at least two-thirds of the commissioners.

5 Stella O. Carpenter, *A Man of Peace in a World at War*, page 207.

6 Report of the Advisory Commission on Constitutional Reform.

7 Clarence D. Wiseman, *A Burning in my Bones*, page 180.

8 Stella O. Carpenter, *A Man of Peace in a World at War*, page 207.

9 Ibid, page 209.

10 Ibid, page 209.

11 Frederick Coutts, *No Continuing City*, page 96.

Chapter Six – Nominees

1 Albert Orsborn, *The House of my Pilgrimage*, page 154.

2 Erik Wickberg, *Inkallad* (Harriers, 1978). English translation, *Called Up* (Salvation Books, IHQ, 2012), page 107.

3 Jarl Wahlström, *En Vallfartssång* (Församlingsförbundets Förlags Ab, 1989). English translation, *A Pilgrim's Song* (Salvation Books, IHQ, 2012), page 100.

4 Henry Gariepy, *General of God's Army* (Victor Books, 1993), page 150.

5 Carroll Ferguson Hunt, *If Two Shall Agree* (Beacon Hill Press of Kansas City, 2001), page 160.

6 John Gowans, *There's a Boy Here*, page 121.

7 John Larsson, *Saying Yes to Life* (Salvation Books, IHQ, 2007), page 200.

8 *High Council 2006*. DVD issued by IHQ.

9 See for example *Mobilized for God: The History of The Salvation Army*, Volume Eight 1977-1994, by Henry Gariepy (The Salvation Army USA Southern Territory), pages 72, 136 and 288.

Chapter Seven – Questions

1 *Constitutional Notes* prepared for the 1939 High Council by Mr William Frost.

2 Wilfred Kitching, *A Goodly Heritage* (SP&S, 1967), page 89.

3 Frederick Coutts, *No Continuing City*, page 100.

4 It has sometimes been wondered whether it would not be better to defer the

election of the members of the Questions Committee until *after* the candidates are identified in order that no one who later becomes a candidate will have been a member of the committee. On this matter High Councils have taken the view that to resolve what some have seen as a potential conflict of interest by reversing the traditional order of events would create larger problems. The procedural and electoral stages of the proceedings would become intertwined and this would have far-reaching consequences. Once the candidates are identified the dynamics of a Council change. Any interventions by them in procedural discussions and especially about the future of the Army would risk becoming part of the electoral process. It is also likely that the duration of the High Council would be further extended. High Councils have furthermore seen it as paramount that the crucial moment of nominations for General should come at a culminating stage in the process of discernment. For these reasons High Councils have preferred to keep to the traditional order of events.

[5] Wilfred Kitching, *A Goodly Heritage*, page 89.

[6] Jarl Wahlström, *En Vallfartssång*. English translation, *A Pilgrim's Song*, page 100.

[7] Frederick Coutts, *No Continuing City*, page 100.

Chapter Eight – Speeches

[1] Letter to Colonel W.F. Jenkins, dated 15 February 1929. USA National Archives.

[2] Erik Wickberg, *Inkallad*. English translation, *Called Up*, page 107.

[3] 1929: Commissioner Edward Higgins – 25 minutes.
1934: Commander Evangeline Booth – not recorded.
1939: Commissioner George Carpenter – 11 minutes.
1946: Commissioner Albert Orsborn – 31 minutes.
1954: Commissioner Wilfred Kitching – 14 minutes.
1963: Commissioner Frederick Coutts – 20 minutes.
1969: Commissioner Erik Wickberg – no speech.
1974: Commissioner Clarence Wiseman – 13 minutes.
1977: Commissioner Arnold Brown – 15 minutes.
1981: Commissioner Jarl Wahlström – 13 minutes.
1986: Commissioner Eva Burrows – 13 minutes.
1993: Commissioner Bramwell Tillsley – 15 minutes.
1994: Commissioner Paul A. Rader – 19 minutes.
1999: Commissioner John Gowans – 8 minutes.
2002: Commissioner John Larsson – 18 minutes.
2006: Commissioner Shaw Clifton – 12 minutes.
2011: Commissioner Linda Bond – 20 minutes.
2013: Commissioner André Cox – 13 minutes.

[4] Stella O. Carpenter, *A Man of Peace in a World at War*, page 215.
[5] Wilfred Kitching, *A Goodly Heritage*, page 89.
[6] Frederick Coutts, *No Continuing City*, pages 97-99.
[7] Arnold Brown, *The Gate and the Light*, page 376.
[8] Jarl Wahlström, *En Vallfartssång*. English translation, *A Pilgrim's Song*, page 101.
[9] Henry Gariepy, *General of God's Army*, page 150.
[10] *Salvationist*, 24 July 1993.
[11] *The War Cry* (USA National), 8 October 1994.
[12] Minutes of the 1999 High Council.
[13] *The Officer*, November/December 2002
[14] *The Officer*, May/June 2006.
[15] *The Officer*, May/June 2011.
[16] Quoted with permission.

Chapter Nine – Election

[1] *Orders of Procedure.*
[2] Frederick Coutts, *No Continuing City*, page 96.
[3] It is in fact highly improbable that a High Council would ever be finally deadlocked, for in a worst-case scenario the General-in-office could, with the consent of more than two thirds of the commissioners, execute a Deed of Variation that would amend Schedule 4 in any way necessary to break the deadlock. Replacing the words 'members present' by 'members voting' would probably suffice.
[4] Frederick Coutts, *No Continuing City*, page 96.
[5] Albert Orsborn, *The House of My Pilgrimage*, page 156.
[6] Clarence D. Wiseman, *A Burning in my Bones*, page 181.
[7] John Larsson, *Saying Yes to Life*, page 201.
[8] Albert Orsborn, *The House of My Pilgrimage*, page 156.

Chapter Ten – Revelation

[1] John Larsson, *Saying Yes to Life*, page 201.
[2] Albert Orsborn, *The House of my Pilgrimage*, page 157. General Orsborn places his words as being spoken after the doors had been opened and 'reporters and cameramen swept in'. But the content of his remarks and the fact that he concludes his account with 'I also read to the Council 2 Corinthians 4' point to this being an account of his private words to the members of the High Council.
[3] Wilfred Kitching, *A Goodly Heritage*, page 91.
[4] *The War Cry*, 21 May 1977.

[5] Stella O. Carpenter, *A Man of Peace in a World at War*, page 218.

[6] Henry Gariepy, *General of God's Army*, page 154.

[7] High Council 2006. DVD issued by IHQ.

[8] Frederick Coutts, *The History of The Salvation Army*, Volume VI, pages 93, 127, 161 and 288. Volume VII (1986), page 73. Also, exceptionally, Henry Gariepy, *The History of The Salvation Army*, Volume Eight, page 304.

[9] Arnold Brown, *The Gate and the Light*, page 183.

[10] Ibid, page 183.

[11] Wilfred Kitching, *A Goodly Heritage*, page 93.

[12] Arnold Brown, *The Gate and the Light*, page 184.

[13] Albert Orsborn, *The House of my Pilgrimage*, page 158.

Index

1929 – a crisis that shaped the Salvation Army's future

John Larsson

'In 1929,' begins the author, 'a constitutional storm that had long been gathering suddenly burst, sweeping from office General Bramwell Booth, the son and successor to William Booth. So traumatic was this event that for many years "1929" – for that is how it was known – was only talked of in hushed tones in Army circles. The telling of what happened was left to those from outside the Army family.'

Now the full story of the crisis, with all its astonishing twists and turns, is set out by a Salvationist writer. In the drafting of this account, General John Larsson (Retired) had access to hitherto unpublished material, much of it in the Army's heritage centres around the world.

'What shook the Army also shaped its future,' concludes the author. 'Through those events of long ago the Army was set on a path of reform that continues to this day. 1929 is part of our heritage.'

384pp (paperback), 28 photographs
ISBN 978-0-85412-794-8
Ebook ISBN 978-0-85412-883-9

Can be purchased from any Salvation Army trade or supplies department and online at www.amazon.co.uk

Saying Yes to Life

the autobiography of John Larsson

World leader of The Salvation Army from 2002 until 2006, John Larsson's period as General was the culmination of a lifetime of service as a Salvation Army officer given in the United Kingdom, South America, New Zealand and Sweden, as well as in influential appointments at the movement's International Headquarters in London. He is the author of a number of books, a widely published composer of music, and the co-writer of 10 musicals.

'My ministry as a Salvation Army officer has been central to my life,' he says, 'but I have not wanted this account to be just an extended version of my officer service record. So I tell the story of the musicals and my other writings, tell of the precious ones the Lord has given me… I touch on events in Salvation Army history that I have lived through or with which I am in some way linked. In addition I leave the door ajar to the hinterland of heart, mind and spirit where I find my inspiration… If I dare call this account *Saying Yes to Life* it is not because I have always succeeded, but because saying yes to life has been my aim.'

264pp (hardback), 55 photographs
ISBN 978-0-85412-760-3

Called Up – Pages from the Story of my Life

the autobiography of Erik Wickberg

The English language edition of the autobiography of Erik Wickberg – the ninth General of The Salvation Army and a testimony to the rich life to be found in the service of God. This book, first published in Swedish in 1978, describes how, having spent his formative years in Sweden, Germany and Switzerland, Erik Wickberg then served as a Salvation Army officer in those countries as well as the United Kingdom. His vast knowledge of languages and thorough appreciation of different cultures stood him in good stead when he was elected to the office of General in 1969. Serving as the Army's international leader for the next five years, he oversaw and visited many aspects of the Army's ministry on every continent. This book provides a moving and colourful account of his life, including fascinating insights into his role as liaison officer in Sweden during the years of the Second World War.

168pp (paperback), 13 photographs
ISBN 978-0-85412-846-4
Ebook ISBN 978-0-85412-872-3

Can be purchased from any Salvation Army trade or supplies department and online at www.amazon.co.uk

A Pilgrim's Song –

the autobiography of Jarl Wahlström

The English language edition of the autobiography of Jarl Wahlström – the twelfth General of The Salvation Army and the first Finnish officer to be elected to that role. In this book, first published in Finnish in 1989, the author describes how, as one of God's pilgrims, he was uniquely privileged to witness the work of The Salvation Army in some of the remotest parts of the world. Jarl Wahlström served as General from 1981 to 1986, and throughout these pages the reader will sense how he thanks God for his pilgrimage and the hope of an eternal goal.

192pp (paperback), 41 photographs
ISBN 978-0-85412-845-7
Ebook ISBN 978-0-85412-871-6